Mt Ararat

CASPIAN
SEA

held
fter

⌂NINEVEH
⌂ HALAH

ASSHUR

MEDIA
where the Ten Tribes of
Israelites were driven into exile
in 722 B.C. and later lost

ELAM

...TAMIA
...rivers"

Tigris river

...YLON⌂

CHALDEA
or BABYLON

⌂SHUSHAN
where ESTHER
was Queen

...ites held
...e 586~536 B.C.

UR
where Abraham
was born

Now
dry land

PERSIA

300   400

...MPIRES

...T EAST

...lan's "Graphic Bible"

PERSIAN

GULF

THE JEWS FROM CYRUS TO HEROD

By

NORMAN H. SNAITH

M.A., D.D. (OXON), HON. D.D. (GLASGOW)

Principal of Wesley College, Headingley, Leeds.

ABINGDON PRESS

NEW YORK ● NASHVILLE

C

PRINTED BY PHOTO OFFSET AND
BOUND BY PARTHENON PRESS
IN THE UNITED STATES OF AMERICA

INTRODUCTION

THIS book was written to serve as a text-book for older scholars in schools and for students in colleges and universities. Most of the chapters are capable of considerable amplification. The student who wishes to study any particular aspect of the period more fully is referred to the Bibliography. Throughout the book an attempt has been made to stream-line everything, to provide the minimum of exact and detailed knowledge which will make the trend of events and the development of ideas plain and intelligible.

This period of Jewish history is of the utmost importance. It is true that where we come from matters, but it is much more important to realise where we are going. A man may be born in a log-cabin, but if he becomes President, we all want to know how it happened. The Hebrews were one of many peoples of the Near East of Semitic stock, but this people became a people of destiny, conscious of divine election. This period from Cyrus to Herod was the cradle of three world religions, Judaism, Christianity, Islam. This is what makes the period so very important, and all the time, from cover to cover, this end (*telos*) has been kept in mind.

NORMAN H. SNAITH

CONTENTS

BIBLIOGRAPHY

Bevan, E. R. *Jerusalem under the High Priests* (Arnold, 1904).

Bevan, E. R. *The House of Seleucus* (Arnold, 1904).

Charles, R. H. *The Religious Development between the Old and New Testaments* (Home University Library, Oxford, 1924).

Clarendon Old Testament: W. L. Wardle, *History and Religion of Israel* (Oxford, 1936); W. F. Lofthouse, *Israel after the Exile* (1928); G. H. Box, *Judaism in the Greek Period* (1932).

ed. T. W. Manson. *A Companion to the Bible* (Scribner, 1940).

Oesterley, W. O. E. *The Jews and Judaism during the Greek Period* (Macmillan, 1941).

Oesterley, W. O. E. and Robinson, T. H. *A History of Israel* (Oxford, 1932). (2 Vols.)

Oesterley, W. O. E. and Robinson T. H. *Hebrew Religion* (Macmillan, 1937).

Robinson, H. W. *Religious Ideas of the Old Testament* (Duckworth, 1923).

Robinson, H. W. *The History of Israel* (Duckworth, 1938).

Robinson, H. W. *Inspiration and Revelation in the Old Testament* (Oxford, 1946).

ed. Robinson, H. W. *Record and Revelation* (Oxford, 1938).

Rowley, H. H. *The Relevance of Apocalyptic* (Harper, 1955).

Rowley, H. H. *The Re-discovery of the Old Testament* (Westminster, (Oxford, 1946).

Snaith, N. H. *The Distinctive Ideas of the Old Testament* (Epworth Press, 1944).

Westminster Historical Atlas to the Bible (Westminster, 1945).

Wright, G. Ernest. *The Old Testament against its Environment. Studies in Biblical Theology No. 2.* (Henry Regnery Company).

PART ONE

THE HISTORICAL BACKGROUND

CHAPTER I

THE RISE OF CYRUS

THE rise of Cyrus was phenomenal. No one expected that a conqueror would ever arise out of those eastern mountains, any more than, centuries later, the Pharisees thought that out of Galilee any prophet could ever come. In early 550 B.C., men had not heard of Cyrus outside Media, and even when he revolted against his Median overlord in that year there was no great concern anywhere else. It was not until another two years or so had passed, and Cyrus had made himself master of both Persians and Medes, that the dealers in high politics took steps to call a halt to the activities of this upstart, thrustful prince. By that time, however, it was too late.

For the beginning of this story we must go back to the death of Asshur-bani-pal in 626 B.C. With the death of this last and greatest of the Assyrian war-lords a new chapter was opened in the history of the Near East. His passing marked the end of an era. For two and a half centuries Assyria had dominated the Mesopotamian valley, and had been a constantly recurring threat to the independence of all the peoples between the mountains of Media and the borders of Ethiopia. When a vigorous king reigned over Assyria, no country was safe. Thrusts were made at intervals until Sargon (722–705 B.C.) captured Samaria, abandoned the attempts of previous kings to govern through a native prince, and made the little that by this time remained of the kingdom of Israel into the Assyrian province of Samarina.

Meanwhile Judah was faithful to her Assyrian overlord, but when Hezekiah joined in a general revolt of the western provinces at the end of the century, Judah was so devastated and such a heavy tribute was exacted that she learned her lesson.   Never again could she be persuaded to join in any attempt to throw off the Assyrian yoke.   This subservient policy preserved Judah as a kingdom, a factor which was of immense importance in the history of the people of God.   It meant that when the Assyrian power did ultimately fail there was still a kingdom which could become independent again, even if only for a few short years.   It gave the king of that day, Josiah, an opportunity to revive the national worship in a way that would have been quite impossible otherwise.   In the north, there was no native Israelite king when Asshur-bani-pal died, and on that ground alone a revival was impossible.   If Judah had rebelled again it would have meant the end of the kingdom, and there could have been no reformation under King Josiah.

When Asshur-bani-pal died, all the subject kings saw an opportunity to recover their independence.   This applies even to Egypt, for Assyria had established her authority even there as early as 671 B.C., though this suzerainty was at best sporadic and always precarious.   The next king was faced with the usual initial problem of re-subduing the kinglets throughout the Empire.   To subjugate Egypt was out of the question, for Asshur-bani-pal had been unable to restore the situation there in 652 B.C.   The new king, Asshur-etil-ilani, found the whole situation beyond his power and ability.   The later years of Asshur-bani-pal's reign had been marked by increasing weakness and growing dissension throughout the empire.   By the time the new king had ousted a usurper his resources were at an end. Nabopolassar had made himself independent in Babylon, away to the south. The general break-up of the empire gave to the kings of Phœnicia and Palestine a freedom for which they had long prayed, but for which they had scarcely dared to hope. It was Josiah of Judah's opportunity, and out of that temporary freedom, five years only after the death of Asshur-bani-pal, there was born the great reformation which we have learned to call Deuteronomic because it was associated with the finding of the nucleus of the *Book of Deuteronomy* during the renovation of the Temple in 621 B.C.

The various small kingdoms regained their long-lost freedom but, even more importantly, there was now a vacant place at the head of the nations. This is why we must go back to the death of Asshur-bani-pal for the beginning of the story of Cyrus. Assyria had occupied this position for a couple of centuries. Who was to succeed Assyria as the dominant power in the Near East? For twenty years there was confusion, with three rivals all longing for the supremacy and none strong enough to stand alone against the rest. Further, even though one of these was eliminated after twenty years, the other two had their spheres of influence, but neither was supreme in the way in which Assyria had been supreme. It was left for Cyrus to establish the Persian power as supreme throughout the whole area, and for him and his successors to extend that power beyond the territories over which even the greatest of the Assyrian kings had ruled. Cyrus's Median-Persian power was the true successor to Assyria. Babylon, for all her greatness, formed but an interregnum.

The three contestants for pre-eminence were Nabopolassar of Babylon, Kyaxares the Mede, and the reigning Pharaoh of the XXVIth dynasty, at first Psamtek II and later Necho. The situation was complicated in the north by incursions of nomads from the steppes of Russia and the highlands of Central Asia. These nomads were the

Scythian hordes who swept down on the Fertile Crescent time and time again during the last quarter of the seventh century.* They saved Nineveh, the Assyrian capital, in 625 B.C., when Kyaxares the Mede was besieging it, but in 612 B.C. they themselves captured the city and sacked it. The remnants of the Assyrian army set up a new kingdom in Haran under Asshur-uballit, but by 608 B.C. or so the whole of the Assyrian resistance had come to an end.

We find Egypt supporting what was left of Assyria from 626 B.C. onwards, probably because the Pharaoh could see that a surviving Assyria was his only hope of maintaining any sort of balance of power against the vigorous and successful Nabopolassar in Babylon. Pharaoh Necho made more than one expedition against the growing power of Babylon, and on one of these excursions he met with Josiah of Judah at Megiddo, in 608 B.C., and there, for whatever reason, Josiah died. Necho marched on to garrison Carchemish on the Euphrates in company with the Assyrians, in an attempt to stop the Babylonian advance up the river, and thence round the Fertile Crescent through Damascus and on to Palestine. But in 605 B.C. Pharaoh Necho was routed at Carchemish. The victor was Nebuchadrezzar, son of Nabopolassar, destined in the next year to become king of Babylon in succession to his father.

This victory is one of the most important in the history of the world. It secured for Nebuchadrezzar the control of the whole of the southern part of the Assyrian empire as far as the borders of Egypt. Meanwhile Kyaxares the Mede continued in power in the north. Each had his own sphere of influence, and the two never came into conflict with each other. Babylon thus had control enough to deport the Jews, but she never succeeded in establishing such a dominant position as that which Assyria had occupied for more than two centuries. The possibility

---

* It is generally held that Jer. *1.* 14f and the whole of the book of *Zephaniah* refer to these invading raids.

of a crash was always present because of the strength of the Medes.

For a little while after the death of Asshur-bani-pal in 626 B.C. Judah had been free, and Josiah had made the most of his opportunities. At his death in 608 B.C., Judah came under Egyptian suzerainty. The people made Josiah's second son, Jehoahaz, king in his stead, but this ruler was *persona non grata* to Pharaoh Necho, who deposed him and installed his brother, Jehoiakim, as king. This was the situation when Pharaoh Necho marched to his doom in 605 B.C. Nebuchadrezzar's victory at Carchemish meant the end of Egypt's power in Palestine, and in due time Jehoiakim became tributary to Babylon.

Egypt was too weak herself to stand up against Babylon, but she was quite capable of stirring up trouble in Palestine, as she had done before, and, also as she had done before, leaving Palestine to pay the price of abortive revolts. In 597 B.C. Jehoiakim revolted against Babylon, undeterred by the earnest protests of the prophet Jeremiah. This prophet knew the history of Israel, if only because he himself was a descendant of the ancient priests of Shiloh. He knew that an unsuccessful rebellion might mean the end of Judah as a kingdom, with no chance of such a revival as Josiah had accomplished, in the far from impossible event of a Babylonian decline from power. Better be satisfied with even a puppet kingship than lose all in a fruitless effort to gain more. Jehoiakim died before the Babylonian armies arrived. He was fortunate, and so was Judah, because his son and successor, the youthful Jehoiachin, surrendered forthwith after a reign of only three months. He went into exile and died there, but the kingdom was saved. Nebuchadrezzar followed the old Assyrian policy. He deported those most likely to cause trouble, left Jeremiah as a steadying influence, and tried to rule the country through a puppet prince, Zedekiah, the third son of king Josiah. But the Egyptians continued to entice

Judah into trouble, and after ten years Zedekiah revolted against Babylon. This was the end of the kingdom, as Jeremiah had feared. The Babylonians came in strength, sacked the city, destroyed the Temple, took Zedekiah captive, put out his eyes, deported yet more people, and left Gedaliah in charge as governor with Jeremiah once more in support. The fate of Israel at the hands of the Assyrians in 722 B.C. was the fate of Judah at the hands of the Babylonians in 586 B.C. There had ceased to be any king in Israel.

The Judæan scene closes with the murder of Gedaliah by a certain Ishmael, who was of royal descent. This Ishmael slew the governor, and with him his Jewish supporters and his Babylonian staff. Gedaliah's chief supporter, Johanan, son of Kareah, was absent at the time, and so survived the massacre. He did his best to avenge his murdered master, but, fearing the Babylonian reprisals, he fled to Egypt, taking Jeremiah with him (Jer. *41.* 11-18). There was a Babylonian expedition in 581 B.C., and a number of people were deported, but after this Judah was humbled and quiet. There was nothing to be done immediately, and in any case Judah was not the one to do it.

The position was not without hope, though there was no immediate prospect of rescue. Babylon was indeed strong, but there were always the Medes, and to these some Jews looked expectantly (Jer. *51.* 11, 28. Isa. *13.* 17). They were wrong, surprisingly wrong. It was not a Median king who conquered Babylon, but Cyrus, this upstart king of Anshan, tributary to the king of the Medes.

In 550-549 B.C. Cyrus revolted against his Median overlord, King Astyages. There seems to have been a fifth column at work, for, at the critical stage of the campaign, so the *Nabonidus Chronicle* tells us, the army of Astyages mutinied, captured him, and handed him over to Cyrus. This made Cyrus king of the Medes. Three years later we find Cyrus styled 'King of the Persians', so the presumption is that in the meantime he had possessed himself of the whole of that kingdom also. This double achievement marks the beginnings of the Medo-Persian empire, destined to become the greatest empire the world had hitherto known. It lasted for two hundred and more years. It was far stronger and more firmly established than ever Babylon had been, and at one time it stretched from the Persian mountains to the borders of Ethiopia and over into Europe.

Nabonidus, the last king of Babylon, was no warrior. His interest was in archæological research, and nothing delighted him more than to lay bare the ruins of days long past. Politically his policy was to preserve a balance of power. Its outcome was the usual outcome of such a policy. There comes a time when the power gets unbalanced, and then whole nations come toppling down. There is some evidence that Nabonidus formed a treaty of friendship with Cyrus, but that was in the very early days before Cyrus grew to his strength. By the time that Cyrus had become king of Media and Persia as well as of his native Anshan, Nabonidus realised that Cyrus was no friend of his, but, on the contrary, a rival with whom he had seriously to reckon. Nabonidus therefore changed his policy, and made a treaty of alliance against Cyrus. His allies were Lydia, Egypt and Sparta, for all four were agreed that it was high time to put a stop to the ambitions of this thrustful prince.

In 547–546 B.C. Crœsus of Lydia opened hostilities and crossed the river Halys, the eastern boundary of his kingdom. After an indecisive battle Crœsus retired to spend the winter in his capital, Sardis, agreeing with his allies to attack Cyrus the following spring. But Cyrus did not wait for the spring. He acted quickly, lest he should find himself forced to fight on two fronts. He followed Crœsus to Sardis, defeated him, and added Lydia to his now rapidly growing empire. The Delphian oracle had told Crœsus that if he crossed the river Halys he would destroy a mighty empire. He did. It was his own.

By this time Cyrus had gained possession of the ancient kingdom of Armenia, a kingdom which had on occasion caused some considerable trouble to the old Assyrian kings. The capture of Sardis thus gave Cyrus control of practically the whole of Asia Minor. Some say that Cyrus immediately turned south to attack Babylon, but the records are scanty for the years between 546 and 540 B.C. It is difficult to estimate his actions. His tactics against Crœsus suggest that he did attack Babylon forthwith. On the other hand, the suggestion of a fifth column at work in the case of Astyages makes it probable that he delayed his main assault on Babylon until he was sure of similar assistance in this greatest of all his adventures. This latter is the more likely, because we know that in his final attack he was assisted by a timely revolt in the far south. Certainly by 540 B.C. Cyrus was master of northern Mesopotamia, and in that same year, according to both Xenophon and Berossus, he was active in western Arabia, where Nabonidus was living in retirement at Tema, pursuing his scholarly interests there, whilst his son, Belshazzar, ruled the empire for him as regent.

The end came soon. In 538 B.C. Cyrus defeated the Babylonian army at Opis on the Tigris, and thus gained control of the irrigation system of canals which was the very life of Babylonia. In the June of that year Babylon opened her gates to Gobryas, whom Cyrus later made governor of the city. In October, Cyrus himself arrived. The neo-Babylonian empire had ended its short-lived life, and Cyrus could add to his titles yet another, King of Babylon.

CHAPTER II

PERSIA

PERSIA instituted a new policy in her treatment of subject peoples, the opposite of that repression which hitherto had been the mode. This previous policy had been to humiliate and to destroy. It involved large-scale deportations as a minimum. In cases of further trouble it involved the deposition of the native rulers and the ruthless destruction of everything in any sense national, including the national religion, for the more national a religion is, the more easily it becomes a rallying-point for all resistance forces.

Cyrus reversed this Assyrian-Babylonian policy of repression, on the sound principle that the happier the lot of subject peoples, the more likely they are to be content to remain subject. Nothing increases resistance like oppression; nothing reduces it like clemency. Cyrus, therefore, gave all deportees the opportunity to return to their native country. He encouraged all peoples to revive their national worship. He even set up puppet princes of the native royal line.

Meanwhile Cyrus himself, fighter rather than administrator, was engaged in campaign after campaign in the east, whilst his son Cambyses governed the empire. Cyrus was killed in 529 B.C., fighting the tribes to the east of the Caspian Sea. Cambyses continued to rule, though now in his own right. Cyrus had been too busy in the east to consolidate his empire in the west. A conqueror of nations is rarely a builder of empires. The task of consolidation therefore fell to Cambyses. It involved the subjugation of Egypt, still active as ever to stir up trouble when she herself was too weak to take any definite military action. Cambyses invaded Egypt in 525 B.C., captured the country, made himself king instead of the reigning Pharaoh, Psamtek III, and became master as far as the borders of Ethiopia. He was still in Egypt when there was a revolt in Persia in 522 B.C. In that year Cambyses died in Haran on his way home. He died by his own sword, some say by accident, others say by suicide. The next years were times of great confusion, but by 518 B.C. Darius I (Hystaspis) had established himself firmly on the throne, and he ruled wisely and well until his death in 486 B.C.

Cambyses had died before he could do much in accomplishing the task of consolidation. What he did not do, Darius did, and he did it uncommonly well. The fact that the Persian empire lasted for over a hundred years after his death in spite of all the disintegrating tendencies of oriental luxury is a lasting tribute to the excellence of his organisation of the empire.

Darius continued the tolerant policy of Cyrus, but he made changes of the utmost importance. One innovation was the establishment of the Imperial Post, by which fast messengers with frequent relays of horses could carry news speedily from one part of the empire to the other. But the most important change was the abandonment of the policy of ruling through native princes. This system had been a great source of weakness in the old Assyrian and Babylonian days, because it meant, more often than not, a general revolt at the death of every king in the hope that the new king might not be able to reassert the imperial authority. It had taken Darius four years to establish himself, and he remembered that for the good of Persia. He divided the whole empire into twenty provinces, each with a satrap domiciled in the principal city. He was careful, however, to make the satrap a civil governor only, whilst the chief of the military in the satrapy was

independent of the governor and answerable to the king
direct. This policy of dividing the responsibility and the
power made it much more difficult for a revolt to take
place. The result was that the consolidation of the empire
could continue from reign to reign without periodic times
of anarchy and confusion. It was this change of policy
which probably accounts for the disappearance of Zerubbabel as governor of Judah, he being a scion of the House
of David. It is true that he was encouraged by both
Haggai and Zechariah to think of striking a blow for
independence. Possibly those are right who think that
Zerubbabel was removed for sedition, and perhaps
executed, but there is no need to make this assumption.
The change of policy which Darius instituted is enough to
account for his disappearance.

So far as the Jews in Palestine are concerned, the reign
of Darius I (Hystaspis) is notable for the rebuilding of the
Temple, the foundation being laid in 520 B.C., and the whole
work being completed by 516 B.C. It is unlikely that there
was any attempt to rebuild the Temple under Shesh-
bazzar in the first days of Cyrus, in spite of the statement
of the Chronicler (Ezra 5. 14–16).

Darius I died in 486 B.C., and was succeeded by his son,
Xerxes I (485–465 B.C.). This is the Xerxes who invaded
Greece and overran Leonidas and his Spartans at Thermo-
pylæ in 480 B.C., only to lose his fleet at Salamis later in
that same year. The story of his father Darius's expedition,
with his defeat at Marathon in 490 B.C., was thus repeated
in the experience of the son. We have no information of
the state of affairs around Jerusalem during the reign of
Xerxes, though we may suppose that the Jews there were
hard put to it to preserve any sort of communal life.

Xerxes was poisoned in 465 B.C., but his third son,
Artaxerxes I (Longimanus, 464–424 B.C.), poisoned the
poisoner and established himself as king after an interregnum of some seven months. His son, Xerxes II, was

murdered by a half-brother after a few months, but once
again the murderer was murdered, this time by another
half-brother, who became king under the style of Darius II
(Nothus, 423–404 B.C.).   He was followed by Artaxerxes II
(Mnemon, 404–358 B.C.), and he in turn by Artaxerxes III
(Ochus, 358–338 B.C.).   One of his most famous generals
was the eunuch Bagoas, who poisoned his master and set
up Darius III (Codomannus, 338–331 B.C.), hoping to rule
the empire through him.   But Darius also knew something about poison, so that once again the poisoner was
poisoned, and Darius pleased himself what he did.   Meanwhile Alexander the Great was marching east, and in the
year 331 B.C. there was fought the last of the three battles
which broke the power of Darius, who fled east to end his
days by the wayside as he hurried through Bactria beyond
the Caspian Sea.

From the Jewish point of view, the three reigns of importance are those of the three kings named Artaxerxes.
Otherwise Palestine continued from reign to reign, prospering in some small degree or not prospering at all, but
in either case without any particular interference from its
Persian master.

Matters reached a crisis in Palestine in the time of Artaxerxes I (Longimanus).   In his twentieth year (445–444
B.C.) there came messengers to the Persian court with news
of great distress in Jerusalem.   They came to the eunuch
Nehemiah, a faithful Jew who was cup-bearer to the king.
The story was one of continual trouble from Jerusalem's
neighbours, who had been taking advantage of the defence-
less state of the city and raiding it when they pleased.
Apparently the inhabitants of Jerusalem had been making
some attempts to rebuild it and so provide themselves with
a measure of security, but these efforts had been brought
to nothing by their enemies.   Nehemiah obtained permission to proceed himself to Jerusalem to establish
security there for his own people.   This he did in spite of

steady opposition both from without and from within the city. He rebuilt the walls, and secured an opportunity for recovery such as Jerusalem had not known since the destruction of the walls by the Babylonians over a hundred years before, in 586 B.C.

In the time of Artaxerxes II (Mnemon)* Ezra the scribe arrived in Jerusalem and instituted considerable changes. Nehemiah had found considerable opposition within the city because of the influential citizens who were on friendly terms with Nehemiah's adversaries, the Samaritans. This faction would do nothing which might antagonise the Samaritans, whereas Nehemiah's party hated the Samaritans and wished to separate themselves with the utmost rigour. The 'separation' party was composed, for the most part, of the returned exiles, who believed themselves to be the true People of God, and held that those who had remained behind in Palestine were but half-bred Jews, and so heathen and apostates. Nehemiah's building of the wall was the first step in that separatist policy which characterised post-exilic Jewry. Ezra's work set the seal on what Nehemiah had forwarded, and at his death Judaism was established, distinct and exclusive. From his time the breach between Jew and Samaritan was inevitable and soon came to be complete.

The reign of Artaxerxes III (Ochus, 358–338 B.C.) is notable for the one revolt in the west against the Persian power. It was occasioned by the failure of Artaxerxes in Egypt. Egypt had been held by the Persians only with the greatest difficulty. They found the problem of maintaining their authority there as difficult to solve as the Assyrians had done. The problem was serious because unless they could control Egypt it was difficult to control

---

* It is now generally agreed that Nehemiah was active from the twentieth year of Artaxerxes I, and Ezra from the seventh year of Artaxerxes II. For a summary of the evidence for this, see OESTERLEY AND ROBINSON : A History of Israel, (Oxford, 1932), Vol. II, pp. 114–18.

Palestine, since Egypt was always seeking to stir up trouble there.   Xerxes I (485-465 B.C.) had had to reconquer the country, but the Persian kings had continued their authority until the time of Artaxerxes II (Mnemon, 404-358 B.C.). He failed to keep Egypt in subjection, both in his campaign of 389-387 B.C. and in that of 374 B.C.   Indeed, towards the end of his reign, in 361 B.C., Egypt even overran southern Palestine.   It was the failure of Artaxerxes III to drive Egypt back which resulted in a general revolt throughout the country.   This was in 351 B.C.   It took the Persian king three years to restore the situation in Palestine, and another two to subdue Egypt once more. What penalty was inflicted on the Jews for their participation in the revolt is uncertain, since our information for the whole of this period is deplorably scanty.   According to Josephus (*Contra Apionem*, I, 184), quoting Hecataeus of Abdera (306-283 B.C.), ten thousand Jews were deported, some to Babylonia and some to Hyrcania, a province of Asia, south of the Caspian Sea, bounded on the east by the river Oxus.

CHAPTER III

ALEXANDER THE GREAT

WHILST the last Persian kings were poisoning and being poisoned, Philip of Macedon was making ready to destroy the now effete Persian empire. He envisaged a united Greece which should dominate the whole world. He therefore sought to entice or to compel all the small Greek city-states into a Hellenic League, which Macedon, though not herself strictly Greek, should lead to victory. But Philip was murdered in 336 B.C. before he could realise his ambitions. These were fulfilled by a greater than Philip, and in a far grander way than ever Philip could have dreamed. His son Alexander, barely nineteen years old, succeeded to the inheritance and to the task.

It was two full years before Alexander was able to march against Persia. These years were occupied by expeditions against the Thracians and beyond the Danube, and by two descents into Greece to enforce the solidarity of the Hellenic League. In 334 B.C. he crossed the Hellespont, and forthwith routed a Persian army of twenty thousand foot on the slopes of Mount Ida by the stream Granicus. It is said that his own losses amounted to sixty horse and thirty foot. This battle gave Alexander the west and south of Asia Minor. He carried Miletus by storm, and left Ptolemy with a thousand men to blockade Halicarnassus, a town in the south-west corner of Asia Minor, opposite the island of Cos. This Ptolemy was with Alexander from the beginning of his campaigns, and after Alexander's death established the most stable of all the empires into which Alexander's conquests were divided after his death. By the time Alexander wintered that first year at Gordium in western Bithynia, he had overrun Asia Minor in the west and south as far as the Taurus Mountains on the western borders of Cilicia.

The next year found Alexander through the pass known as the Cilician Gates and into Syria. There, in October 333 B.C., he out-generalled and completely defeated Darius III (Codomannus) at Issus, north of the Orontes and not far from the coast of the Gulf of Alexandretta (Iskanderun). Alexander marched south. Tyre held out for seven months until July 332 B.C., Gaza for two months, and Alexander entered Egypt, there to be greeted as saviour and deliverer.

In the spring of 331 B.C., Alexander left Egypt, and in the October of that same year he sealed the doom of the Persian empire at the battle of Gaugamela, which is east of the Tigris and north of Nineveh. This gave him Mesopotamia, but he marched east, and next spring hurried north after the fleeing Darius, missed him by eight days at Ecbatana, and so, onward through the Caspian Gates into Bactria, where he found Darius dead by the roadside, slain by his own people.

Succeeding years found Alexander beyond the Oxus and even beyond the Indus, till in June 323 B.C. he died of a fever in Babylon, after the prolonged drunken orgies which, according to the old Macedonian fashion, marked the funeral feast in honour of Hephaestion, the friend of Alexander's youth. Alexander had been king for four months less than thirteen years, and he was not yet thirty-three years old. The territory he had overrun was vaster than that which had belonged to Persia even in Persia's palmiest days. His conquests are of the utmost importance because they involved the spread of Greek ideas and Greek culture generally, and this to an extent that cannot be over-estimated. These ideas formed the basis of that eastern Mediterranean culture which Rome took over from the second century B.C. onwards. This became the basis of the Roman civilisation, and in turn it has formed the framework of our modern western world.

For all this we have to thank Aristotle. The most important thing that Aristotle ever did was his going to the court of Philip of Macedon in the year 343 B.C. to be tutor to the young prince, Alexander, then thirteen years old. This boy had already learned to love the old Homeric poems, and his first tutor, Lysimachus of Acarnania, had encouraged him in boundless ambitions even to believing himself a son of the gods. It was left to Aristotle to mould him into the man he became. Aristotle gave to the young Alexander a tremendous love for all things Greek— literature, art, beauty, language, everything. Above all he imbued him with a great admiration for the Greek style of government. Aristotle was himself expert in the study of political institutions, none more so in his day, nor indeed any as much. The result of all this was that when Alexander set out to conquer the world he was moved not only by the personal ambitions which he owed to Lysimachus, but also by a strong desire to make real those dreams of the Kingdom of Man which Aristotle had implanted in him. When his soldiers, either through wounds or through age, could not keep up those tremendous forced marches which were in part the secret of his success, he discharged them in groups. The veterans settled where they were discharged, married native women, and raised their families. But each settlement was modelled on the Greek pattern, a small cameo of Greece in a barbarian land. By this means a common culture was established from east to west and down into Egypt, and it was a Greek culture. It came about, therefore, that even though Alexander's empire broke up into many pieces at his death, yet every piece was Greek. It mattered not whether Syrian or Egyptian ruled in Palestine, for both Syrians and Egyptians were apostles of the Greek way of life.

This is the way in which, to use Dante's phrase, Aristotle came, for the Middle Ages, to be 'the master of them that know'. It was not primarily through his many writings. These, many of them unpublished and some of them unfinished, were in the possession of his disciple, Theophrastus. He bequeathed them to a certain Neleus, whose heirs in Asia Minor buried them in a vault to prevent them from being seized by the king of Pergamos for his new library. There they lay, safe but forgotten, till Apellicon the Athenian bought them for his library. This was about the year 100 B.C. The writings came into the light of day when Sulla seized them and brought them to Rome in 86 B.C. Then it was that the scholars of Rome were able to study Aristotle's works *in extenso*, and the complete edition of his works by Andronicus of Rhodes belongs to the year 50 B.C. Aristotle's reputation was thus not created by his written works, but rather enhanced. He had already been established as Master through the general Greek culture which Alexander had spread. The fact that Aristotle's work is still largely the basis of our modern thinking is thus due primarily to Alexander's conquests and the consequent spread of Greek language and culture. This took place long before his many writings came to be sedulously studied and copied in Rome during Cicero's time.

Aristotle once said: 'The Greeks might govern the world, could they but combine into one political society.' Here is the genesis of Alexander's aim and method. This was the task Alexander set himself to accomplish, but the idea was Aristotle's, and to this day Aristotle rules the world.

CHAPTER IV

PTOLEMY AND SELEUCUS

ACCORDING to Josephus (*Ant. Iud.*, XI, VIII, 3), Alexander turned aside to Jerusalem on his march south to Gaza and on to Egypt. The story is that Alexander himself offered sacrifice in the Temple 'according to the direction of the High Priest'. The incident is probably wholly fanciful, but all the traditions suggest that Alexander was well disposed to the Jews. The effect of Alexander's conquests, however, is not discernible amongst the Jews until the period after his death, when his generals and their descendants strove with one another for pre-eminence.

Alexander died without having made any proper provision for the administration of the many countries which he had overrun. The chiefs of the Macedonian army, therefore, met together after his death in order to decide what was to be done. The choice for the succession lay between Alexander's half-witted half-brother, Philip Arrhidaeus, and the unborn child (if it should prove to be a boy) of Alexander's Bactrian wife, the princess Roxane. The foot soldiers supported Philip. They were Macedonian peasants, who loved the rough Macedonian ways, and disliked those oriental splendours which had changed the Alexander they had loved. The more oriental Alexander had become, the more they had grown tired of the ceaseless marching even further and further east. It was this tiredness of his foot soldiers which had made Alexander call a halt in his victories. The cavalry preferred to wait until Roxane's child was born. They themselves belonged to the upper classes, and they took kindly to the luxuries and the splendours of the East. Perhaps, too, the leaders were hoping that the delay would give them opportunity to win a kingdom for themselves when the empire broke up.

In the end a compromise was effected, and it was agreed that both Philip and Roxane's son should rule, with Perdiccas as regent. Perdiccas had been one of Philip of Macedon's generals, and he did his best, but it was a task beyond the power of any man. Alexander's generals shared the satrapies amongst themselves. They began each one to consolidate his own position, and soon they were banding themselves together against Perdiccas.

Matters came to a head when Antigonus, satrap of Phrygia, refused to obey Perdiccas. This meant war, with Perdiccas and Eumenes, who had been Alexander's chief secretary, fighting against four of the generals. Perdiccas himself attacked Ptolemy in Egypt, and sent Eumenes to deal with the other three. This was the Ptolemy whom Alexander had left to subdue Halicarnassus with a thousand men whilst he himself had marched on. He had been the first of the generals to see which way the wind was blowing when Alexander died. He chose Egypt for his satrapy, a wise choice, because it was by far the easiest to hold. It was less accessible, its frontiers by sea and land formed a natural protection, and it gave him command of the sea. As soon as the trouble started he stole Alexander's body and carried it off to Egypt, thus, in popular thought at any rate, forwarding his claim to be the true successor to Alexander.

Things went from bad to worse with Perdiccas in his campaign against Ptolemy, till finally his army and his generals revolted, and Perdiccas was slain. But amongst these generals, and indeed their leader in the revolt, there was a young man named Seleucus. During Alexander's latest campaigns he had been one of Alexander's favourite and most successful generals. He had not received a satrapy in the general share-out, but had taken the command of the Macedonian cavalry under Perdiccas, as offering more opportunity for advancement so long as the regency prevailed. But the events of 321 B.C., ending with the mutiny and the death of Perdiccas, convinced him of his error. Henceforth Seleucus was to be numbered amongst the generals who strove for the mastery. He abandoned his cavalry command and set off east to establish himself as satrap of Babylonia.

At first Seleucus found his position one of extreme difficulty. There was a time when he was a fugitive, but later the tide turned for him, and by 311 B.C. he had made himself indisputably master in Babylonia. This is the date which his successors regarded as the beginning of the Seleucid era.

The whole period from the death of Perdiccas in 321 B.C. to the battle of Ipsus in Phrygia in 301 B.C. was a time of confused anarchy, of ever-changing alliances between the contestants, and of ceaseless marchings to and fro. But the battle of Ipsus did something to clear the ground. At this battle there were three against one. There should have been four, and the absence of that fourth had a great deal to do with the subsequent course of Jewish history. The one was Antigonus, who at that time held the whole of Asia Minor. The three were Lysimachus, who had held Thrace ever since the original partition, Seleucus, now master of Babylonia, and Cassander, who had made himself master in Macedonia. The fourth was Ptolemy of Egypt, but he was absent overrunning Coele-Syria (Palestine), his agreed share of the spoils in the event of victory. Antigonus was defeated and slain. Seleucus added Syria to his possessions. He and his allies, those who had indeed fought at Ipsus, declared that Ptolemy's absence rendered the agreement null and void, and that Coele-Syria should now be given to Seleucus. Seleucus went to take it, but found Ptolemy in possession. Ptolemy had always been anxious to control that territory, as every ruler of Egypt has been throughout the centuries, and he had gained and lost it more than once during the time of Antigonus's supremacy. Seleucus, finding Ptolemy in possession, expressed himself in the oft-quoted terms preserved by the historian Diodorus (xxi, 5): 'He would not take any action for the present, for friendship's sake, but later on would consider the best way of dealing with a friend who grasped more than his share.' In this incident there began a rivalry between the descendants of these two generals, Ptolemy and Seleucus, by which each line sought to possess Palestine. The struggle lasted, off and on, for more than a century, and was to have tremendous influence on both the history and the religion of the Jews.

The battle of Ipsus in 301 B.C. left five main contestants still in the field, but with Seleucus (Babylonia and Syria) more powerful than ever before, he having to a large extent succeeded to the dominant position which the dead Antigonus had held. Ptolemy was still strong in Egypt and Palestine. The other three were two of the victors of Ipsus, Cassander (Macedonia) and Lysimachus (Thrace), and Demetrius, son of Antigonus, who had managed to hold on to parts of Asia Minor and the whole of the Phoenician coastline. Twenty years later, in 281 B.C., Seleucus managed to get possession of the territories of these other three, thus making himself master of the whole of Alexander's empire except Egypt and Palestine, which Ptolemy held. He crossed into Europe to take possession of Macedonia, the land of his birth and still the best-loved land of all. On his way thither, soon after crossing the Hellespont, he was murdered. The year was still 281 B.C.

The sudden death of Seleucus on the very eve of the fulfilment of his crowning ambition brought considerable confusion, and Antigonus Gonatas, son of Demetrius, managed to gain control of Macedonia. We are thus left with three powerful kingdoms, each of them sufficiently strong to maintain itself against either of the two others, or indeed even against a combination of the other two. The year 276 B.C. finds these three empires firmly established, each dominant in its own continent. The House of Seleucus was controlling Babylonia, Syria, and Asia Minor. Its capital was Antioch by the mouth of the Orontes, the city which Seleucus had built in honour of his father Antiochus, who had risen to honour under Philip of Macedon. The House of Seleucus was thus paramount in Asia. In Europe the House of Antigonus was in control. In Egypt the House of Ptolemy was strong, with the first Ptolemy not long dead. He had predeceased his rival Seleucus by a couple of years or so (died 283–282 B.C.). This general situation with its three strong kingdoms lasted until Rome marched east in the first years of the second century B.C., and in course of time subdued them one after another.

Since the year of the battle of Ipsus (301 B.C.) the Ptolemies had been in control of Palestine, but the sons of Seleucus never rested until the country was theirs. There were periods of trouble between 276 and 240 B.C. Seleucus II (Kallinikos, 246/245—226/225 B.C.) even attempted to drive Ptolemy's men out of Palestine. He was heavily defeated and there was peace for twenty years.

Throughout the century the Jews were properly submissive to their Greek-Egyptian masters, and were treated well. There was considerable literary activity during this time. It is probable that *Chronicles, Ezra-Nehemiah* were written in these days. Probably also many of the psalms were edited and incorporated into the Psalter, and there was also great activity amongst the wise men who contributed to the formation of the *Book of Proverbs*. The good relations existing between Jews and Greek-Egyptians provided also the occasion for the beginning of the translation of the Hebrew Bible into Greek (the Septuagint).

With the accession to the Seleucid throne of Antiochus III (the Great, 223–187 B.C.) the tempo quickens. This vigorous king very soon made an attempt to conquer Palestine, but was beaten back. He made a second attempt in 219 B.C. and for two years all went well, but in 217 B.C. he was utterly routed by the Egyptian armies at Raphia, on the extreme southern border of Palestine, near to the coast, and south-west of Gaza. Ptolemy IV (Philopator, 221–203 B.C.) thus regained Palestine and retained control of the country for the rest of his life.

The next king was a child of four, and with the regency there came intrigue at court and political weakness. This gave Antiochus the Great his chance, and he took it. By 199 B.C., Palestine was his, and the Ptolemies had lost their hold on Palestine for ever. Thus the great-great-grandson of Seleucus fulfilled the threat of the first of his line and wrested Palestine from the great-great-grandson of Ptolemy, the 'friend who grasped more than his share' For the Jews, it meant that their time of quietness was over, for soon oppression was to take the place of gentleness.

CHAPTER V

PALESTINE UNDER THE SELEUCIDS

IT may very well be that Antiochus the Great and his successors were not designedly harsh in their treatment of the Jews, though the recurrent difficulties of these kings of Antioch may have disposed them to harsh measures at the slightest sign of provocation. It has to be said, however, in justice to them, that the provocation was far from slight, and that many kings would have been as exasperated as they with less justification.

Unfortunately for Antiochus, no sooner had he consolidated his position in Palestine than he found himself in conflict with Rome. He was largely enticed into this by Hannibal, the life-long enemy of Rome. When Hannibal was defeated at Zama in 202 B.C., in Carthage's last stand, he fled east and found refuge at the court of Antiochus, there to stir up what further trouble he could against the Rome he had fought since he was a youth. There had been unrest in Greece. The Aetolians had quarrelled with Rome, and wanted help. Antiochus, encouraged by Hannibal, was ready to respond. He invaded Greece. His task was all the easier because Rome had vacated Greece, sedulously carrying out her promise to make Greece free. The lust of conquest had not yet become a vital factor in the foreign policy of Rome.

This invasion of Greece by Antiochus the Great marks a change in the affairs of the eastern Mediterranean. It roused Rome to a new activity, with a determination this time to see the whole thing through to the end. In 192 B.C. Rome declared war on Antiochus, and the next year the Roman armies marched into Thessaly. Antiochus sought to hold the pass of Thermopylae, and once more that mountain track brought disaster to the defenders. The resultant slaughter meant the end of Antiochus's adventures into Greece, but, worse still, it was not the end of Rome for Antiochus. Hannibal warned Antiochus that Rome would follow him now into Asia.

And so there began a new page in Roman history, for this campaign taught Rome that there was wealth and luxury in conquest. Previously Rome had fought for her life. Now she began to fight for power and wealth. In 190 B.C. Cornelius Scipio, with his brother Africanus as his lieutenant, defeated Antiochus at Magnesia, half-way between Sardis and Smyrna. At Magnesia the Romans lost four hundred men. Antiochus lost fifty-three thousand. He had to give up all Asia except Cilicia; he had to pay an enormous indemnity for twelve successive years; he had to surrender his elephants and his navy; he had to agree to surrender Hannibal and other refugees from the might of Rome. Hannibal fled, but the remainder of the terms were ruthlessly enforced. Henceforth Rome was always a threat to the Seleucid kings of Antioch, and therefore also a force to be reckoned with in the politics of Palestine.

There is another factor to be noted so far as the events of the next generation are concerned. The younger son of Antiochus the Great was a hostage in Rome for the payment of the indemnity. This younger son, who afterwards became king under the title Antiochus IV (Epiphanes, 175–163 B.C.) spent twelve years in Rome, for whose might he gained a healthy respect, so that years later, when the Roman authorities warned him to leave Ptolemy alone, he withdrew without more ado lest a worse thing befell.

These Seleucid kings found themselves in perpetual conflict, either with enemies outside of the State, or with their own relations within it. Wars cannot be fought without money and plenty of it. This was all the more so because of the great sprawling empire over which these kings ruled. It came about therefore that the need for money became more than ever a major factor in Antiochus's administration of the provinces. It is probable that the Jews were at first well treated by Antiochus III (the Great), if only for the reason that he had trouble enough on his hands elsewhere without raising a hornet's nest in Palestine. Indeed Josephus has much to say concerning the extreme generosity of the Seleucid king to his new subjects. It is true that they had to pay heavy taxes, though Josephus says that all the Temple personnel were exempt. Be that as it may, the Jews were used to paying heavy taxes to the Ptolemies, that being the one respect in which it might be said that the rule of the Ptolemies had been oppressive. When the Romans laid this heavy indemnity on Antiochus, the king's need for money became desperate in the extreme, and his demands caused complications in Palestine.

This heavy taxation is important because it had as much as any other one thing to do with the reasons for the Maccabæan revolt. The story of the trouble goes back to the time of Ptolemy IV (Philopator, 221–203 B.C.), when Onias II, the High Priest, refused to pay his personal tribute tax to Ptolemy. This refusal was just before the battle of Raphia, when there was every indication that Antiochus III (the Great) would defeat Ptolemy and drive him right out of Palestine, and so retain the country permanently. The tax amounted to twenty talents of silver—between four and five thousand pounds sterling according to pre-1914 standards. It is probable that this sum was paid annually by the High Priest in return for receiving the royal recognition. But Joseph, the leader of the rival faction in Palestine, managed at this time to be appointed tax-farmer for the whole

c

country instead of for Judæa only. This involved a great increase of power and wealth for Joseph's party, the House of Tobias, and it raised the House of Tobias to be at least as powerful in the land as the House of Onias. It has been suggested that Joseph's success in the matter of the taxes was connected with Onias II's quarrel with Ptolemy, but this supposes that Onias was defaulting in respect of the taxes. This can scarcely be the case. In the first place, the sum of twenty talents was comparatively small, and would fall far short of the amount of taxes for the part of the country which Joseph gained. In the second place, the taxes were farmed out. The nobility went to Alexandria, and the right to collect the taxes was sold to the highest bidder. Joseph, we may suppose, offered more than anyone else, and so obtained the right to collect all the taxes for the whole country.

It therefore came about that when Antiochus the Great conquered Palestine the Tobiads (i.e. the sons of Tobias) held all the tax-collection rights. Joseph continued in this office, and became pro-Syrian. When Onias II had refused to pay his tax to Ptolemy, Joseph had curried favour with Egypt. The positions were now reversed. The Tobiads became the pro-Syrian family, and the Oniads pro-Egyptian. The enmity and rivalry between the two factions grew steadily worse, perhaps all the more easily because Joseph was actually a nephew of Onias II, whose sister had married into the other family.

In 187 B.C., Antiochus the Great died, and was succeeded by his son, Seleucus IV (Philopator, 187–175 B.C.). During his reign his chief minister, Heliodorus, attempted to seize the Temple treasure with the connivance, it was alleged, of Simon, the eldest of the four sons of Joseph the Tobiad, though he accused Onias II, the High Priest. These sons of Joseph caused a great deal of trouble in Jerusalem. The three eldest were always at loggerheads with Hyrcanus, the youngest, who was Oniad in sympathy.

To such a pitch did the disturbances in the city grow that Onias III, grandson to Onias II and High Priest at the time, went to the Seleucid court to get help from the king in order to quell the riots. Whilst Onias III was away, Seleucus was murdered (175 B.C.) by Heliodorus, and his brother, Antiochus IV (Epiphanes, 175-163 B.C.), became king. Meanwhile Jason, Onias's brother and a pro-Syrian, bribed the new king, Antiochus, and got himself appointed High Priest in the room of his absent brother. The priestly aristocracy were largely Hellenist in their sympathies, and were prepared to make many concessions in respect of Jewish customs in order to keep on good terms with the ruling power. Jason excelled them all in this zeal. He even sent three hundred silver drachmæ, about a hundred and sixty pounds sterling, for the worship of Herakles-Melkart, the god of Tyre. The messengers themselves asked that the money should be expended on the fleet (2 Macc. 4. 20, margin), but it is perhaps not altogether surprising that a High Priest who had obtained his office through bribing a Gentile king should regard such a gift as consistent with his loyalty to Jehovah. But such conduct did not ultimately avail Jason, for after three years a certain Menelaus offered Antiochus a bribe larger by three hundred talents than that which Jason had given, and Menelaus became High Priest. Jason fled into the Ammonite country, which was probably the ancestral home of the Tobiads, that is, if they were indeed descendants of that Tobiah the Ammonite who had been so active in Nehemiah's time, two and a half centuries before.

Menelaus committed two crimes which made him cordially hated by all Jews who loved the Law. He had actually been unpopular from the beginning, since he was not of the high-priestly family at all. Jason, indeed, was never regarded by the orthodox as being the true High Priest. They clung to Onias III in their loyalty. But Jason, being own brother to Onias, was at least of the true family. As for this Menelaus, he was a rank outsider, and his appointment was an impossible one so far as the orthodox were concerned. Menelaus's first crime was to secure the murder of Onias III, the true and rightful High Priest. His second crime was to instigate his brother Lysimachus to steal the holy vessels in the Temple.

As if there were not yet troubles enough in Palestine, there came a rumour that Antiochus had been killed, fighting in Egypt. This was in 169 B.C. Jason thereupon reappeared in Jerusalem, drove Menelaus out, and murdered such of his supporters as he could lay his hands on. But the rumour of Antiochus's death was exaggerated. He was very much alive, and he returned from Egypt in great wrath, doubly great because of two untoward happenings, one of which had nothing at all to do with the Jews. In the first place, the Romans had warned him off Egypt, and, as we have seen, Antiochus had seen enough in his youth of the Roman power to make him think twice before he made his father's mistake and measured swords with Rome. In the second place, this driving out of his nominee, Menelaus, could scarcely be construed by him as anything less than rank insolence. Everything was all the more exasperating because he had been compelled to withdraw from Egypt just when he was justified in thinking that at last he had Egypt within his grasp.

Whatever Antiochus's ultimate reasons were, he was fully determined to clear up the whole Palestinian situation once and for all, and to teach those rebellious, factious Jews a lesson they would remember for many years to come. He was not the first, nor has he been the last, to be driven to extreme measures because of disruptive action by the Jews in Palestine. Probably there was another factor so far as Antiochus was concerned. Rome had barred him from any territorial expansion in the west when she drove his father out of Asia Minor. She now barred any extension in the direction of Egypt. There was little

hope of any further developments east of Babylonia. It
was all too far away. Indeed, the Seleucid kings did very
well to hold on to their eastern possessions, let alone advance
any farther into the Persian and Median mountains.
Where Antiochus could not extend, he could at any rate
consolidate. No eastern empire has ever suffered from
too much consolidation. He therefore embarked upon
a Hellenising policy as never before. According to
1 Macc. *1*. 41f, he sought throughout his whole kingdom
to impose a common culture and religion. In the case
of the Jews this involved an attempt to stamp out their
religion altogether, and to substitute for it Gentile customs
in general and the worship of Zeus and the Greek deities
in particular. Outside Palestine Antiochus succeeded
without any great difficulty; indeed there is every indication that already a common culture and religion had been
established elsewhere. In every country there are always
those to be found who will hurry to ingratiate themselves
with the ruling power, however alien that power may be.
There was a strong and enthusiastic Hellenising party
even within Jewry, and this had its central core in the
priestly aristocracy, of all people.

It will be seen that there were many influences at work
which rendered it both desirable and necessary for Antiochus Epiphanes to set about determinedly to uproot the
Jewish religion. He abolished the Jewish sacrifices. He
set up heathen altars and caused swine's flesh to be offered
on them. He even placed an altar to the Olympian Zeus
on the very altar of the Temple itself. Anyone found with
a copy of the Law was punished with death. Many Jews
submitted, but gradually the opposition grew more and
more stubborn. Very many Jews were put to death.

The climax came when the Greek officers came to
Modein, a village in the hills between Jerusalem and Joppa.
There they required the aged priest Mattathias to sacrifice
to the heathen gods on an altar which had been set up

locally. He refused. Another local headman stepped forward to make the sacrifice. Mattathias struck him down and slew him over the altar. He followed this up by killing the officer and destroying the altar. Then he fled to the hills, his sons and his followers with him. To this little band there flocked all who were zealous for the Law. They made every effort to strengthen the Jewish resistance, both by encouragement and by threats. 'They smote sinners in their anger, and lawless men in their wrath; and the rest fled to the Gentiles for safety.'

A clash between the rebels and the king's troops was inevitable. It took place on a Sabbath, when a small body of Jews was trapped. They refused to fight or even to defend themselves, seeing that it was the Sabbath. They were massacred, men, women and children. This untoward incident led the orthodox and rebel Jews to resolve to fight even on the Sabbath, if it were a matter of defending themselves. About this time the resistance groups were joined by the Chasidim, a group of men whose zeal for the Law was paramount. Their fanaticism knew no bounds. They soon became the backbone of the fight for religious freedom. The name 'Chasidim' means 'faithful, devoted ones', and where the word occurs in the Psalter it is translated 'pious ones', 'saints'. These were the men who for more than a generation had formed the opposition to the priestly aristocracy who had supported the Hellenising ways of the Seleucid kings. They were not strictly a political party, but joined in the revolt because it was clearly a religious revolt. Later, when religious freedom had been achieved, they refused to fight on for political freedom. For this reason, chiefly, the rebels later met with disaster. The fanatical nucleus of the rebels had gone.

Mattathias soon died, and the third of his sons (Josephus says he was the eldest) became the leader. This was Judas, surnamed 'Maccabæus', which probably means 'the Hammerer'. He managed to unite all the guerilla groups under his command. He was indeed the perfect guerilla chief. The Seleucids were unable to deal with the rebellion with what troops they had in Palestine, and these local bands were time and again swept away by Judas. He routed the local Syrian-Greek leader, Apollonius, and followed that victory up by surprising a larger force under Seron in the pass of Beth-horon. It was clearly time for Lysias, left in charge of the west whilst Antiochus Epiphanes was away in the east, to take more serious steps to quell the revolt. He sent an army under Nicanor and Gorgias to advance against Judas, who was in the Judæan hills. They encamped on the edge of the plain by the valley of Ajalon. Gorgias, with one-eighth of the force, attempted to surprise the camp of Judas by night, but Judas became aware of the plan, so that Gorgias found the camp deserted. Meanwhile Judas fell suddenly on the rest of the army in Nicanor's camp, and swept them headlong across the plain with Gorgias's men also involved in the rout. This battle probably took place in the summer of 164 B.C. According to 1 Macc. 4, it was a year earlier, and that authority talks of another successful engagement in the next year, this time against Lysias himself. It is probable that 1 Macc. is in error here, and that the fight with Lysias was later, and by no means successful. In any case, after the victory of the summer of 164 B.C. Judas obtained a respite, and he took advantage of it to restore the Temple, cleanse it of every pollution, and reinstitute the Temple services according to the Law. This rededication took place in December, 164 B.C., and its memory is preserved to this day in the Jewish Festival of Chanukkah (Dedication). Thus the fight for religious freedom was won, and the Temple worship restored. The first phase of the wars of Judas the Maccabee was ended.

But there were other Jews in trouble from the Gentiles,

men in Gilead and in Galilee. They appealed to the
successful Judas for help, so Judas and his brother Jonathan,
the youngest of the five sons of Mattathias, went to Gilead,
whilst Simon, the second son, went into Galilee. They
rescued the faithful and brought them into Judæa. Judas
now began to grow more and more sure of himself and of
his destiny. He made expeditions into Philistia, into Edom
and to the east of Jordan generally. More important still,
he began to dream of political power also.

All along Judas had been helped considerably by what
was happening elsewhere in the Seleucid empire. The
king had his hands too full to spare many troops to deal
with what to him was a series of minor disturbances.
When, however, it became plain that Judas was seeking
further worlds to conquer, Lysias the governor was forced
to turn his attention once more to Judas and this time
with greater seriousness.

When Antiochus had set out for the east he had appointed
Lysias regent and had made him guardian of his seven-
year-old son, the heir to the throne, the boy Antiochus
(later Antiochus V, Eupator). But for some strange
reason, when he was on his death-bed, he appointed one
of his generals, Philip, to be both regent and guardian.
Perhaps the historian Polybius was right in saying that the
king was 'supernaturally deranged', for he certainly could
have done nothing more calculated to cause trouble and
civil war. There is a fair amount of evidence that in view
of this situation Lysias was prepared to let well alone, and
was quite willing to let the Jews have their way over the
matter of religious freedom and a reasonable amount of
independence generally. But Judas was not content.
He had been able to restore the Temple worship. He had
managed to assert his authority beyond Judæa, but he had
never been able to turn the Syrian garrison out of the
Akra, the citadel which overlooked the Temple. Judas
now believed himself strong enough to deal with this

matter, so he set about trying to starve them out, but some escaped his blockading forces, and aided by Seleucid sympathisers amongst the Jews they sent for help to the boy king, who was in Lysias's charge.

Lysias knew that sooner or later he would have to deal with his rival-regent, Philip, but he thought he had just time to deal with Judas before Philip could detach himself from events in the east. As it happened he had just not time enough; but at first all went well. Judas soon found himself in difficulties. Lysias attacked from the south up the valley through Beth-zur. He was held up there, but he detached a force to invest the fortress, and himself marched on. Judas attacked him at Beth-zacharias, but was driven off and had to retreat. Here it was that one of the five brothers died. All were killed in time, either in battle or by murder, but Eleazar was the first. He was the fourth of the five brothers, and was crushed by an elephant he killed, believing it to be carrying the young king. Judas found himself shut up in the Temple fortress with a mere handful of supporters, and it seemed as if the end had come. But by this time Philip had arrived, and Lysias had to finish off his Judæan campaign in order to be free to meet his greater enemy. Judas received better terms than even the wildest imagination could conceive. He received a full pardon and complete religious freedom. Menelaus, the High Priest, was put to death, and Judas was recognised as the king's representative in Judæa. He had to submit to the destruction of the Temple fortress, and to the continued Seleucid occupation of the Akra. It was agreed that prayers and sacrifices should be offered in the Temple for the king's majesty.

When Menelaus had been deposed from the high-priesthood and put to death a certain Jakim had been installed in his stead. This Jakim, better known by his Greek name, Alkimus, was of the true Aaronic stock, but was pro-Syrian (Seleucid) in his sympathies. Judas soon drove Alkimus out because of his pro-Syrian attitude. Alkimus appealed for help to Demetrius, the king's cousin, who had set himself up as a rival king. Demetrius sent one of his generals named Bacchides with a substantial force. Judas was driven out of Jerusalem and Alkimus was reinstated, being willingly received by the Chasidim. This group had formed the spearhead of Judas's fight for religious freedom, but they were zealous only for the Law, and thought now that Judas was zealous for other things. They found a High Priest of the true Aaronic descent quite acceptable, especially since he promised to let bygones be bygones. But Alkimus broke his promise and massacred them, a very foolish thing to do.

This time the expedition was entrusted to Nicanor. According to the Jewish histories, Nicanor sought to follow Alkimus's policy of feigning friendship, but Judas suspected the truth and fled to the hills. There is, however, some justification for the opinion that they became good friends, but that their friendship was broken up by Alkimus, who found such a friendship inconvenient to the highest degree. Whatever it was that actually happened, Nicanor one day appeared in the Temple, demanding with vehemence that Judas be surrendered to him, and threatening to destroy the Temple and to build a heathen temple in its place. But Judas was away in the hills gathering men for the fight. This took place at Adasa in the pass of Beth-horon on the 13th Adar, early in the year 160 B.C. Nicanor was slain, and the Day of Nicanor became an annual festival amongst the Jews, marking the death of the man who had presumed to challenge the Most High God in the very Temple itself. This was Judas's last victory. An army came to avenge the fallen general. Judas was brought to bay with his army dwindled to no more than eight hundred men. His alternatives were to fight or to run away. He preferred to stand and fight, and he fell. This was at Elasa, an unknown site, probably away to the north of Jerusalem. The

month was April, some two months after the defeat of
Nicanor, and the year was 160 B.C.

Following the death of Judas the nationalist movement
fell on evil times. The three surviving sons of Mattathias
were driven out of the country, and they fled across the
Dead Sea marshes into the desert. One of the brothers,
John, was killed in some obscure affray, but the other two
brothers, Jonathan and Simon, slowly built up their
strength in the hope of renewing the conflict. In time
Jonathan managed to make himself virtual ruler of the
countryside, whilst the Syrians held all the strong points.
This was the time of rival contestants for the Syrian throne,
a time of bewildering changes of policy, with the Egyptian
kings interfering to make confusion worse confounded.
The two surviving sons of Mattathias made the most of
their opportunities, and made the best bargains they could
with the various rival contestants. Jonathan grew from
strength to strength till he made the fatal mistake of
listening to the fair words of the usurper, Tryphon. He
enticed Jonathan into the city of Ptolemais, he and a
thousand men with him. Tryphon massacred the thousand,
imprisoned Jonathan, and finally put him to death beyond
Jordan. The last of the five brothers now took up the
struggle. This was Simon, the second son. Simon
managed to secure good terms from Tryphon's rival, and
from this date, 142 B.C., he secured complete immunity
from taxation. This date was held by the Jews to be the
beginning of their independence. In the next year, in
May, 141 B.C., the garrison in the citadel of Akra surrendered, and Simon entered Jerusalem with songs and
praises and great rejoicing.

All went well with the Jews until the spring of 135 B.C.,
when two events took place which transformed the whole
scene. This was the third year of Antiochus VII (Sidetes,
139/138—129 B.C.). This king was the last king in whom
the energy and determination of the first Seleucids shone

forth. In that year he began to take steps to restore the full Seleucid power in the west. The Jews had never previously been able to stand up against the whole might of the Seleucid kings, and they failed now as before. In that year also Simon was murdered in his cups by his son-in-law, Ptolemy, who had invited him to a carousal. But Simon's son, John Hyrcanus, heard of the plot in time to rush from Gezer to Jerusalem before Ptolemy could get there. And so John Hyrcanus became High Priest and ruler of the Jewish State.

John Hyrcanus soon found himself in great difficulties. He was hemmed in within the walls of Jerusalem, and the siege began in earnest. When food grew short, Hyrcanus expelled the numerous non-combatants from the city, but Antiochus refused to let them through his lines. Then the time of the Feast of Tabernacles came round (the year was 134 B.C.), and Hyrcanus was forced by shame to let them into the city again. Antiochus was not only powerful; he was wise. He proclaimed a truce during the Feast and himself sent offerings. By a combination of obvious military strength and statesmanlike actions he brought Hyrcanus to sue for terms. These were severe enough from the military point of view, but otherwise they were characterised by the utmost generosity. He disarmed the Jews, and broke down the walls which they had built for their defence. He also demanded rent for cities outside Judæa proper, but otherwise he required neither tribute nor indemnity. He even waived his original demand for the establishment of a garrison in Jerusalem, and accepted instead five hundred talents of silver with hostages. He then marched away east, taking Hyrcanus with him, but leaving behind him a well-satisfied people. The Seleucid authority continued in Palestine until the death of Antiochus Sidetes in 129 B.C. That date marks the end of Seleucid enterprise in Palestine.

CHAPTER VI

HIGH PRIEST AND KING

WHEN Antiochus VII (Sidetes) died in 129 B.C., John Hyrcanus was able to take steps towards the recovery of his former freedom. We do not know when he returned to Palestine, but he was there when his opportunity came. He found himself with practically a free hand, because the rest of the story of the Seleucid kings is almost entirely an account of rival claimants and continual fighting between them. They were all far too busy to interfere with John Hyrcanus. He extended his power in all directions, in Central Palestine, beyond Jordan, and in Idumæa. Those who were in the conquered countries were given the alternatives of either embracing the Jewish faith or of emigrating. He made many converts. He died in 104–103 B.C., having some considerable time before that assumed the title of King. He had 'administered the government in the best manner for thirty-one years', so says Josephus in his *Antiquities of the Jews* (XIII, x, 7). He was succeeded by his son, Aristobulus I, who reigned for one year only, but extended his father's conquests to include at least part of Galilee.

Aristobulus was the eldest of five brothers. He imprisoned three of them lest they should oust him from the high-priesthood, and shared the government with the other, Antigonus. But Salome, wife to Aristobulus, was a dangerous and determined woman. She drove a wedge between the two brothers, and finally caused Antigonus to be murdered. Then, when Aristobulus died, she released the three brothers, and married the eldest of them,

Alexander Jannæus, making him both High Priest and King.

Under Alexander Jannæus the Jewish kingdom was still farther extended. He conquered Gilead, most of the Ammonite country and of the Moabite country, and all the south away to the borders of Egypt. The first two years of his reign (he reigned from 102/101—76/75 B.C.) were thoroughly and completely chaotic, what with rival Seleucid kings and Egyptian rivals interfering in Palestine also. Ultimately everyone seems to have got tired and gone home. Alexander was left master in Palestine, and then it was that he began to make headway, east and west and south.

If his internal affairs had gone as well as his external affairs, everything would have been well, but this was far from being the case. These were the times when the rivalry of Pharisee and Sadducee came to a head. The trouble had really begun years before in the time of his father, John Hyrcanus, when that ruler adopted the title of King. This was the cause of serious offence to the Pharisees, who held that God alone was King. In their zeal for the Law these Pharisees were true descendants of those Chasidim whose fanaticism had brought success to Judas Maccabæus sixty years or so before. Josephus tells us (*Antiquities*, XIII, x, 5–6), that Hyrcanus gave a great feast, and professed his ardent love for all things in accordance with the Law. He requested them to tell him if he in any way offended, whereupon a certain Pharisee, Eleazar by name, asked him to give up the high-priesthood and content himself with the civil power only. When asked why, Eleazar replied that rumour had it that Hyrcanus's mother had once been a captive in the time of Antiochus Epiphanes. The inference was that she had suffered the usual fate of captive women and had been violated, and that therefore her son, being the son of a woman who was impure, was ineligible for the high-priesthood. Tempers began to rise, and a Sadducee who was present, by name Jonathan, sought to make party capital out of the situation by pointing out to Hyrcanus that he could soon see whether all the Pharisees agreed with Eleazar by asking them what punishment ought to be inflicted upon him for this insult. Jonathan succeeded beyond his wildest dreams. The Pharisees suggested only the most lenient of punishments, and a breach was made between Hyrcanus and the Pharisees. Henceforwards Hyrcanus was hand in glove with the Sadducees. Things were no better under Aristobulus, who also assumed the title of King, the real cause of offence to the Pharisees.

Under Alexander Jannæus things went from bad to worse, for he added crime to crime. He started with a crime, for he married Salome, Alexandra Salome, as she came to be called after this marriage. It was against the levitical law that a priest should marry any but a virgin. The levirate law did not apply to priests, who were in fact definitely prohibited from marrying the deceased brother's widow. Things were not improved by the obvious fact that Alexander was not only a warrior, but more than ordinarily ambitious in this respect. Yet again, there is ample evidence that he went out of his way to flout the proper regulations for the ritual during his observance of his high-priestly office at the Feast of Tabernacles, with the result that on one occasion the people pelted him with their citrons. Alexander completely lost his temper and ordered his soldiers to attack the people, with the result that many Jews were slain in the Temple courts. So virulent did the hatred grow that Alexander Jannæus had to depend more and more upon foreign troops in his wars, and there was a time when there was civil war for six years. The tradition is that he finally crushed all opposition, when he captured the Jews who still held out against him, crucified them, and caused the throats of their wives and children to be cut whilst they were hanging there. Truly an unlovely man, though he was High Priest and King. He had no more trouble in the land for the rest of his reign.

When Alexander Jannæus was on his death-bed (76-75 B.C.) he advised his wife, Salome, to make peace with the Pharisees. This she did, and she appointed her elder son Hyrcanus II to be High Priest whilst she held the civil authority. During her time (75/74—67/66 B.C.) the Pharisees became very powerful. Practically the whole of the religious and civil administration came to be in their hands. Both Salome and her son, Hyrcanus, were definitely in sympathy with them. The younger son, Aristobulus, was Sadducæan in his sympathies. As the years passed by, the Pharisees grew more and more arrogant, and they began in time to try to pay off old scores. The result was that Sadducæan opposition grew apace, fostered by Aristobulus, whose disposition was far from being as quiet and retiring as that of his brother, Hyrcanus. Already, before Alexandra Salome died, Aristobulus had determined on action, and as soon as she did die in 67-66 B.C. he appeared with an army and defeated his brother near Jericho. Hyrcanus willingly retired in favour of his more active brother, who became High Priest and King until 63 B.C.

All might have gone peacefully enough, with Hyrcanus in retirement and Aristobulus as High Priest and King, if it had not been for the governor of Idumæa, whose name was Antipater, the father of Herod the Great. This Antipater had a father bearing the same name, who had been appointed governor of Idumæa by Alexander Jannæus. When the father died, the younger Antipater had succeeded to the position. Antipater was in part afraid for himself lest Aristobulus should drive him out of Idumæa and even worse things befall him. But chiefly Antipater was a man of action and ambition. He finally persuaded Hyrcanus into action, and between them, with the help of the fire-brand Nabatæan King, Aretas III, they defeated Aristobulus and shut him up in Jerusalem.

At this stage of proceedings Rome interfered for the first time in Palestine itself. This was in the person of Pompey the Great. Roman policy by this time had changed from the beginning of the previous century, and Rome was now definitely out for conquest and power. The defeat of Antiochus the Great had opened the eyes of the Romans to the possibilities of world dominion and the luxury and wealth involved. Here was Pompey, busy achieving renown in the east, whilst Cicero and Cataline at home were contending rivals for the consulship. Pompey heard of the troubles in Palestine whilst he was in Syria, and sent his general, Scaurus, south to secure what advantage he could for himself and for Rome. Both sides offered him bribes, but Aristobulus was the highest bidder, so Scaurus supported him. He ordered Antipater, Aretas and Hyrcanus to withdraw, whereupon Aristobulus followed them up and signally defeated them in battle.

The next year Pompey ordered them to appear before him, so that he could settle the dispute once and for all. He said he would deal with Aretas first, and settle the Jewish dispute afterwards. In reality he had come to the conclusion that Aristobulus was completely untrustworthy, so he turned suddenly against him, besieged him in Jerusalem, and finally broke into the Temple, where Aristobulus and his supporters made their last desperate stand after a three months' siege. Twelve thousand Jews died, and Aristobulus was carried off a prisoner to Rome. Pompey himself marched into the Holy of Holies, but took no spoil from the Temple, leaving everything as it was before. Hyrcanus found himself once more High Priest, but ethnarch instead of King, tributary to Rome for a country that included Judæa, Galilee, Idumæa, and Peræa. Antipater was the real ruler until he was murdered in 43 B.C.

D

CHAPTER VII

HEROD AND ROME

THE years between 63 B.C. and 43 B.C. were troubled years for all the eastern world, especially the last ten of them. The year 54 B.C. marked the estrangement of Cæsar and Pompey. From 49 B.C. there was civil war between Cæsar and Pompey, till Pompey was defeated at Pharsalus in Thessaly in 48 B.C., and later murdered in Egypt. Then Cæsar was murdered in 44 B.C., and there was war between Brutus and Cassius on the one side and Mark Antony and Octavian (later Augustus Cæsar) on the other. The first stage of the conflict ended with Antony master in the east, and Octavian in Italy and the west. It was during the confusion which followed the death of Cæsar that Antipater was murdered.

Antipater and Hyrcanus had plenty of troubles during these twenty years, apart from those in which they were involved as part of the Roman Empire. Aristobulus was still alive, and he had by this time two sons who were as restless and ambitious as their father. But one way and another Antipater got rid of his enemies, mostly through being a firm supporter of Pompey. In 48 B.C., when Pompey fell, Antipater found himself on the wrong side. He lost no time, however, in changing over. After the murder of Pompey, he sent reinforcements to Cæsar in Egypt, persuaded the Egyptian Jews to support Cæsar, and generally did everything he possibly could in his usual thorough-going fashion to secure Cæsar's triumph.

In Antipater's whole-hearted support for Cæsar there began a friendship which brought great benefit to the family of Idumæan Antipater and so to the Jews also. Cæsar's kindness to the Jews was most màrked. He did everything possible to conciliate the Jews, and everything possible to strengthen the hand of Antipater. He recognised the Jews as an *ethnos*, that is, a definite race with its own ruler, though tributary to Rome. Taxation was remitted. The Jews were permitted to have their own courts of justice in which all offences could be tried except such as interfered with the rule and overlordship of Rome. Jews were not to be enlisted into the imperial armies, and the Roman legions were withdrawn from Judæa. This was almost like freedom, but Cæsar had to take corresponding steps to ensure loyalty to Rome and to minimise the chance of rebellion. This he did by strengthening the position of Antipater in every possible way. He was fully confident of Antipater's loyalty, and he trusted him completely. He did well, for no Roman who trusted either Antipater or his son, Herod the Great, ever had any reason to regret his action. Cæsar made Antipater governor of Judæa, and granted him the status of Roman citizenship with all that this implied as to Rome's help in time of trouble. Antipater was even permitted to rebuild the walls of Jerusalem. Cæsar's clemency to the Jews extended to Egypt and to the whole of the Dispersion. When Cæsar was assassinated, the Jews lost the best friend they had ever had.

But in spite of all the benefits which Antipater secured for them, the Jews hated him with virulence. Time and again Jewish history has been marked by a strange perversity by which the Jews have in course of time antagonised their best friends. This happened with both Antipater and his son Herod, and with Rome also. Their hatred for Antipater was on two counts. Partly, it was because he held Judæa for Rome, the foreign power, when the Jews as a nation longed for the establishment of a theocratic state in which God alone would be King. And further, on the same ground, there was no doubt about Rome's being master. Former overlords, whether Persian, Seleucid or Ptolemaid, had held the reins somewhat loosely, with a typically Oriental slackness. But Rome was western, and there was nothing of this about Roman rule. The Roman legions were disciplined and thorough in ways which no Oriental despot had ever been able to achieve. But most of all, and this was the second ground of offence, Antipater was an Idumæan, a descendant of the hated sons of Esau, that Edom which the Jews hated with a more-than-ordinary hatred.

It thus came about that in the end Antipater reaped a bitter reward for all he had done for the Jews. It happened when Cassius came into Syria after the death of Cæsar and established himself there in strength. He exacted the money he needed with considerable brutality and ruthlessness. The consequent resentment of the Jews was concentrated on Antipater. Things had not been going too well for Antipater for some two or three years. For one thing, he was getting older, and the years of continued anxiety and watchfulness were taking their toll. He had delegated the authority round Jerusalem to his elder son, Phasael, and that in Galilee to his younger son, Herod. Herod immediately started securing order in Galilee, and rounded up the brigands who infested the countryside. One of the foremost of them, a certain Ezekias, he captured and summarily executed. For this he earned the heartfelt gratitude of the common people, but the Jews of Jerusalem saw a chance to create trouble. They accused Herod of acting illegally since it was the Sanhedrin alone which had the right, under Jewish law, of life and death in such a case. Hyrcanus, still High Priest, was forced to summon Herod to appear before the court. Herod came and his guard with him, but when he saw how the land lay he fled to Damascus to seek the protection of Sextus Cæsar, the new governor. Sextus supported him, and Herod was barely prevented by his father and his elder brother from descending upon the Jews with an army and exacting vengeance. But Herod had a long memory, and when his day came he remembered this to the no small discomfort of his enemies in Jerusalem. All these quarrels added fuel to the fire, so that the exactions of Cassius made things very difficult for Antipater. In the end he was poisoned through the plots of a rival, but Herod soon had him revenged when the murderer himself was stabbed to death. This took place in 43 B.C.

The next year, 42 B.C., was the year of the battle of Philippi, when Cassius and Brutus were defeated by Antony and Octavian. The Jewish leaders, Hyrcanus, Herod and Phasael, had all been supporters of Cassius, not with the enthusiasm with which Antipater had supported Julius Cæsar, but rather perforce, since Cassius had made himself master in Syria. All three hurried forthwith to secure Antony's goodwill, and so did Hyrcanus's nephew, the son of that Aristobulus who had caused such trouble in earlier days until Pompey dealt with him. Antony confirmed Hyrcanus in his high-priesthood, and made Phasael and Herod joint tetrarchs.

During the next five years the fortunes of the House of Antipater reached their nadir. Antony needed money badly, and Phasael and Herod had to get it out of the Jews. Antony neglected political affairs because of his infatuation for Cleopatra. The Parthians appeared on the scene from the faraway east. Things could scarcely have been worse for Phasael and Herod. That rival nephew, Antigonus by name, bribed the Parthians with money and women. With their help he easily possessed a willing Jerusalem, and captured Hyrcanus and Phasael. Hyrcanus was deposed and carried off to Babylon where, however, he was treated with respect. Phasael was imprisoned and committed suicide by dashing his head against the walls of his cell. Herod managed to escape. He went to Rome in sorry plight, and begged the kingdom for the grandson of

Hyrcanus, the son of Hyrcanus's daughter, Alexandra. Herod's idea was to rule the kingdom through this grandson, the young Aristobulus, just as his father Antipater had ruled through Hyrcanus. Herod had married Mariamne, Alexandra's daughter; so this young Aristobulus, whose claims he had gone to Rome to favour, was his brother-in-law.

Herod arrived in Rome with everything lost except his courage. To his astonishment, Antony and Octavian made him King of Judæa, and promised him help in restoring the situation in Syria, where the Parthians were now in control. These Romans knew how to pick their men. After many vicissitudes Herod managed to straighten matters out. In 37 B.C., after a three-months' siege, and with Roman help, Herod captured Jerusalem, beheaded Antigonus, and set about securing order in his unexpected kingdom. This was the time when he remembered those men who had tried to eliminate him over that trouble concerning the executed brigand in Galilee. Herod forthwith executed forty-five of them. He needed the full support of Rome if he was going to maintain his position, so he levied heavy taxes on the wealthy and gave the money to Antony. Apart from these necessities, both of them essential for his own safety and continued well-being, Herod did his best to create better relations between himself and the Jews, but the hatred which they bore him was too great thus to be overcome. Nothing could alter the fact that he was an Idumæan, a descendant of the hated Edomites. He still held the country for Rome. He still was possessor of the rule and the authority which belonged to the Hasmonæans. And he had a speedy and effective way of dealing with opposition.

For twelve years, down to 25 B.C., Herod had unceasing trouble. This was caused almost entirely by the women, his own womenfolk and Cleopatra. Alexandra, his mother-in-law, never forgave Herod for being made King by the Romans instead of her own son, Aristobulus. The fact that Herod had not himself sought to oust Aristobulus made no difference to Alexandra. Herod was King, and that was enough for her.

Alexandra, beyond doubt, was a most determined woman, and her zeal for her son, Aristobulus, knew no bounds. She completely dominated Mariamne, her daughter and Herod's chief wife, whom Herod loved most passionately. Further, there was Cleopatra in Egypt, fully determined to win back all that her father had lost in Palestine. She never ceased to seek concessions there from her lover, Antony. Antony found himself perpetually in a strait betwixt the two. He could not hold Syria without Herod, and he was enchained by Cleopatra. Herod seems to have been one of the few men who were not blinded by Cleopatra's charms. Perhaps Cleopatra never forgave him for this. The story is long and involved, and it ended in the execution by Herod of all the conspirators. Aristobulus was drowned whilst bathing in 35 B.C., at the age of seventeen. Herod was summoned to appear before Antony over this incident, Antony being forced to take action by Alexandra and Cleopatra. When Herod returned home, having cleared himself with Antony, he found a hot-bed of trouble, which resulted in the execution of his uncle, Joseph, whom he had left in charge, and the imprisonment of Alexandra, whilst Mariamne narrowly escaped execution. Later on, he executed both Alexandra and Mariamne, as well as his sister Salome's husband. But this was after the battle of Actium in 31 B.C.

This year of 31 B.C. brought Herod much-needed relief. Antony was defeated at the battle of Actium, and Cleopatra committed suicide. But the downfall of Antony left Herod in a position of considerable difficulty, since he had been a most loyal supporter of Antony in good times and bad times alike, and that in spite of everything that Cleopatra could do. Herod did what his father, Antipater,

had done in similar circumstances. He went boldly to
Octavian at Rhodes. There, instead of fawning before
the conqueror, he proudly boasted of his loyalty to the dead
Antony. He regretted that he had not done more for
him, and suggested that if it had not been for Cleopatra
he would have been able to do more. He said that he
had been Antony's friend right to the end, even when
things were going badly for him. Herod finished his speech
by saying that he was a man who could be loyal to his
friends, and that if Octavian would receive his friendship
he would be as loyal to Octavian as he had been to Antony.
Octavian knew a man when he saw one. He confirmed
Herod in his kingdom of Judæa, gave him a territory as
large as that of Alexander Jannæus had been, and all was
well between Herod and Rome.

It was when Herod got back home that he found the
situation worse even than when he had had to appear
before Antony to answer for the death of the young
Aristobulus, and it was on this occasion that he determined
to make an end of the whole business. This was when
he executed Mariamne, his wife, and his governor,
Sohemus, and when, having discovered still more plots,
he executed also Alexandra, his mother-in-law, and his
sister Salome's husband.

For eleven years Herod was left in peace, but the last ten
years of his reign, from 14–4 B.C., saw the old family feuds
resumed. Herod became an embittered and murderous
old man. He had never been slow to liquidate persistent
plotters. Now he had three of his sons executed, and he
became thoroughly ruthless and cruel, all the more easily
because in his later years he was afflicted by a painful,
incurable disease. But whatever Herod the Great did, he
kept the peace for Rome. He was clever, personally
ambitious, a born ruler, but first and foremost loyal to
Rome. That, in any case, was where his main interest
lay. He knew well enough that without the power of

Rome behind him he would be able to do nothing. Rome knew, too, that without Herod she could never hold Syria. Octavian had been right when he took Herod at his word at Rhodes, and he never had the slightest cause to regret his action. Herod was a great builder; he conferred numerous benefits on the Jews, but they hated him with a hatred that never died. The fact that he did so much to renovate and beautify the Temple passed for next to nothing. He was still an Edomite, and he kept the peace for Rome.

We come now to the period of the earthly life of the Lord Jesus Christ. The details, therefore, of the lives of the sons of Herod the Great are of considerable importance.

According to Herod the Great's will, his kingdom was to be divided between his three sons, Archelaus, Antipas, and Philip, but Archelaus was to be king. These dispositions needed confirmation at Rome, especially the matter of the kingship, for Rome admitted no hereditary kingship anywhere in the empire. All three brothers found their way to Rome, with Archelaus and Antipas seeking the kingdom, and Philip supporting Archelaus. In addition there was an embassy of Jews who wanted to be rid of the sons of Herod altogether, and to come under the direct rule of Rome. 'A certain nobleman went into a far country, to receive for himself a kingdom, and to return. . . . But his citizens hated him, and sent an embassage after him, saying, We will not that this man reign over us' (Luke *19*. 12–14). The result of all these representations was in accordance with Herod's will, except that Archelaus received the title of ethnarch only, with a partial promise of the kingship if all turned out well. Thus Archelaus was ethnarch of Judæa, Samaria and Idumæa; Antipas was tetrarch of Galilee, Peræa and Jewish territory east of Jordan; Philip was tetrarch of the area east and north of the Sea of Galilee.

But things did not turn out well for Archelaus. He was

unpopular from the first, and he added to his unpopularity steadily from year to year. Even before he had gone to Rome to be confirmed in his position there had been trouble in Jerusalem, and Archelaus's troops had massacred three thousand Jews at the Feast of Passover. The situation was so precarious that the Syrian legate, Varus, had deemed it wise to come nearer to Jerusalem with his three legions, a thing no Roman would ever have dreamed of doing if Herod the Great had still been alive. There would have been not the slightest need. But the Romans did not behave with their former wisdom and integrity. Sabinus, the proconsul, sought to appropriate Herod's property. Varus prevented this, but when Varus had restored peace in Jerusalem he left a legion behind to maintain it, and retired to Antioch. Sabinus thereupon robbed both the palace and the Temple treasury. This meant more trouble and bloodshed.

Archelaus certainly had a difficult situation with which to deal, some of it, though by no means all, of his own seeking. As soon as Herod the Great was dead all the pent-up hatred of the Jews against his family burst forth. Archelaus was the least equipped of Herod's sons to deal with the situation. This grew steadily worse, partly because of its inherent difficulties, but partly also as a result of various actions on the part of Archelaus which were bound to upset the Jews. He divorced his wife and married his deceased brother's widow. He forcibly removed the High Priest on two separate occasions, and generally behaved in a barbarous and high-handed manner. The upshot was that the Romans listened to the representations of the Jews, exiled Archelaus to Gaul, and governed Judæa through a procurator. The first procurator was Coponius (c. A.D. 6–9).

The first three procurators seem to have governed the country wisely. We know nothing of any untoward happening until the procuratorship of Valerius Gratus

(A.D. 14–26). There had been trouble in Galilee during the time of Coponius, when a census was undertaken by the Syrian legate, Quirinius. Judas of Gamala had revolted, and the revolt became serious, mostly because of predatory bands of rough fellows who roamed the countryside. Rome put down the revolt, but it set a bad fashion, and was the first of a series of disorders which ended with the destruction of the Temple and the extinction of all Jewish political hopes in Palestine. In Judæa there was no trouble, chiefly owing to the wise counsels of the High Priest, whose name was Joazar.

Valerius Gratus was responsible from A.D. 14 onwards for sowing those seeds of ferment and exasperation which grew to make the final clash of A.D. 66–70 inevitable. The next procurator, Pontius Pilate, was rather worse. He was unwise where he might easily have chosen the other way and been right, and he was stubborn when he was in the wrong. The growing ferment perhaps made these procurators less careful than they might have been otherwise; and it is certain that acts calculated to lead to exasperation were not all on one side. This was the period of the *sicarii* (the dagger-men), and by murder and sabotage they strove to render organised government in Judæa impossible. In the end the Samaritans appealed to the legate, and Pilate was removed from office. The year was A.D. 36.

By this time the end was practically inevitable. There was a grandson of Herod the Great, whose name was Herod Agrippa I. He had been sent to Rome by his grandfather to be educated, and obtaining entrance to the highest circle in Rome, had grown up to be an expert in enjoying himself. He was a close friend of Claudius, and when Claudius became emperor in A.D. 41, he added Judæa and Samaria to the territories which Herod Agrippa was already supposed to be ruling. This gave Herod Agrippa the whole of the territories over which his grandfather, Herod the Great, had ruled. Agrippa did everything he could to please the Jews. This was for far more than reasons of policy. He was genuinely interested in the welfare of the Jews, thoroughly good-humoured, and generally conciliatory in attitude. Unfortunately he died in A.D. 44. If he had lived longer he might have done a very great deal to improve the relations between Jew and Gentile.

He left a son, of the same name, who in time succeeded to a position of authority. He neither had the wisdom of Antipas, who had ruled so well in Galilee for over forty years, nor had he the good-humouredness of his father. He was genuinely interested in the proper preservation of Jewish customs and in the proper observance of the Law (Acts 26. 3), but he made many mistakes, and these, though they might have passed a generation earlier, were now regarded by the Jews as serious. When the procurator interfered he made matters worse. The land grew more and more unruly. First, there was enmity between Jew and Gentile, made no less by a growing Jewish arrogance on the score that they were the People of God who kept the Law. Next, there were lawless bands who infested the country. This lawlessness was most exasperating to the procurators, whose duty it was primarily to keep order. Further, there were the extremists, the Zealots, who, either independently or as terrorist groups, sought by murder and assassination to precipitate the crisis. As the years passed by the procurators found it more and more difficult to distinguish between sects and parties, until finally they gave up trying to be particular. Added to all this, there was the religious fanaticism which grew more intense with every Roman attempt to put down sedition.

The new procurators who were in charge after the death of Herod Agrippa I had a difficult position with which to deal. The first was Cuspius Fadus. He met with nothing but trouble, and had to deal with a false Messiah, Theudas,

whom he beheaded. The next procurator had to deal
with the great famine. His successor got involved in a
dispute between the Jews and the Samaritans, was over-
ruled by the emperor, and relieved of his post. This
meant that the Jews won their case, and they were thereby
encouraged to be awkward with the procurator. Felix
and Festus both did their best, but they made mistakes,
though the Jews also contributed their share to the steady
deterioration of the situation. In the time of Florus, the
Zealots got the upper hand and broke out into open revolt.
The leaders of the Jews, both Pharisees and Sadducees,
besought Herod Agrippa II to put down the revolt. But
it was too late. The situation was out of hand, and the
war began in A.D. 66. At first the Jews met with success.
The proconsul, Cestius Gallus, tried to storm the Temple
buildings, lost many thousand men and was driven off.
This victory increased the ardour of the Zealots, who saw
in it evidence of the favour of God. By A.D. 67, however,
Vespasian had reduced Galilee, and by the middle of
A.D. 68 most of Judæa had been conquered. Then Nero
died, and Vespasian was busy elsewhere. When he
eventually became emperor he sent his son, Titus, to make
an end of Jewish resistance in Jerusalem. This was in
A.D. 70. Titus captured the Temple after a siege of five
months.

During the whole period of two years while the Romans
had been inactive there had been continual strife and
bloodshed between the Jewish parties. This continued
even when Titus was before the walls. In the end the
survivors combined forces to meet the Romans and fought
to the end, the last stand being made within the very
Temple itself. Then finally the Romans set fire to the
Temple. The two leaders, John of Gischala and Simon
Bargoria, managed to escape from the flames, and continued to fight with a few Zealots in the upper city. Some
few escaped, and the rest died fighting.

PART TWO

THE RELIGIOUS DEVELOPMENT

CHAPTER VIII

THE RESTORATION

THE Jews who came back from the Babylonian Exile were thoroughly and completely convinced of three things. These three things were the determining factors in the whole subsequent development of Judaism, both politically and religiously.

Firstly, they were sure that there was One God and that there was none other than He, supreme in wisdom and in power.

Secondly, they were sure that they, and they alone, were the chosen people of this One and Only God; they were the true Israel.

Thirdly, they were sure that this One God would see to it that they, His chosen people, would accomplish a glorious destiny at the head of the nations.

All these three themes are set forth plainly and vigorously in the writings of 'The Second Isaiah', that unknown prophet of the Babylonian Exile whose work is found in the sixteen chapters, Isa. *40-55*. Everything subsequent to 538 B.C. revolves around these three themes. On their consciousness of their unique destiny the whole story of the post-exilic Jews depends.

I. THE ONE GOD.

It is in the writings of the Second Isaiah that the religion of Israel first becomes clearly and explicitly monotheistic.

Such a belief had doubtless been implicit as far back as Moses. Such a prophet as Amos in the middle of the eighth century B.C. had reached out to a faith that was monotheistic for all practical purposes. Strictly speaking, however, the religion of the Hebrews up to the time of the Exile was henotheistic, that is, they worshipped one God, but did not deny the existence of other gods. Jehovah was the God of Israel, but Chemosh was the god of Moab, Milcom of the Ammonites, and so forth. Each god had his own territory and his own people. David, driven out of his homeland by Saul, could say: 'They have driven me out this day from joining myself with the inheritance of Jehovah, saying, Go serve other gods' (1 Sam. 26. 19). Similarly, Naaman, the Syrian general, believed that if he had enough Israelite soil to stand on he would be able to worship Israel's god, even though he was far away in Assyrian territory (2 Kings 5. 17f). Something of the same type of thought is to be found even in Mic. 4. 5: 'For all the peoples may (or 'will') walk each one in the name of his god, but as for us, we will walk in the Name of our God for ever and aye'—a passage which may not be from the hand of eighth-century Micah himself but is certainly not earlier.

Yet these eighth-century prophets are closer to monotheism than Mic. 4. 5 would suggest. Amos, for instance, thinks of Jehovah as controlling the destinies of peoples other than the Israelites. He brought Israel out of Egypt, but He also brought the Philistines from Caphtor (? Crete) and the Syrians from Qir, away beyond Damascus (Amos 9. 7). In the series of oracles in the first two chapters of the *Book of Amos*, the power of Israel's God extends in judgement to such neighbouring countries as Damascus-Syria, Philistia, Ammon and Moab. Isaiah of Jerusalem can speak of Assyria, mighty though she be, as the rod of Jehovah's anger (Isa. 10. 5), and can continue to speak of Israel's God as sending that country on its destructive errand.

But whilst we find indications in these eighth-century prophets that they regard Jehovah's power as extending beyond the confines of Israelite territory, yet the full monotheistic doctrine of the One and Only God is not set forth by them. This full flower blossomed in Babylon, where the exiles found themselves in the midst of a people who claimed that their chief god, Marduk, was creator of the world, holder of the tablets of destiny, and arbiter of all things to come. Against these claims the exiles found themselves consciously working out in detail what had been implicit in their religion from the time when Moses spoke to them of the God who had brought them out of the land of Egypt. This God, as Ezekiel told them, is bound by no place, and wherever His people are, and are in need of Him, there is He. Seated on His chariot-throne, He had come to them in the whirlwind out of the north (Ezek. *1*), leaving, though loath to leave, that Jerusalem which He loved (Ezek. *10*. 4; *10*. 19; *11*. 23; *10*. 20).

This God, who could traverse the deserts to come to the banks of the river Chebar, is Master of all Nature. He alone created the heavens and the earth, measured out the waters in the hollow of His hand, meted out the heavens with the span of it, and contained all earth's dust in His own small tierce-measure (Isa. *40*. 12). He calls forth the stars every night, and they rise at His bidding, every one of them in its turn (*40*. 26). He alone stretched out the heavens, and spread the earth beneath them (*44*. 24; cf. also *45*. 18; *48*. 13).

He is immeasurably superior to man. His thoughts are not our thoughts, neither are His ways our ways. 'For as the heavens are higher than the earth, so are my ways higher than your ways, and my thoughts than your thoughts' (*55*. 8, 9). All nations are as nothing before Him (*40*. 17). He can make even the proud Babylonians into fugitives (*48*. 14), and bring Babylon to the dust, captive, naked, and humbled before the conqueror

(*47*. 1-3). Egypt and Ethiopia are but pawns in His hand, and with them He can bargain for the prosperity of Israel (*43*. 3f). Humbly they shall come to Israel and fawningly bow down to them (*45*. 14). Then there is that Cyrus, the new conqueror who has been carrying all before him in the north; even he has been raised up by Jehovah, though all unwittingly, to do His bidding; for Cyrus is an anointed one of Jehovah, chosen for the special purpose of setting God's people free (*45*. 1-5).

But it is for the idol gods of Babylon and those who make and worship them that this prophet reserves his greatest scorn. What blind fools they are, those wealthy ones who take a graven image and have it overlaid with gold and garlanded with silver chains (*40*. 19); or those poorer ones who take a block of hardwood and seek a craftsman to turn it into an idol which they fondly hope will stand firm for ever! Most ridiculous of all those who plant a fir-tree, and when it has grown its height, use part of it to roast flesh, part of it to keep themselves warm, and the rest to make a god of it, to bow down to it, and to pray to it to save them (*44*. 14-17). Bel and Nebo, gods of Babylon, were wholly powerless to save even themselves. They had to be tied on to the backs of beasts of burden, and were so heavy and helpless that both beasts and gods were captured (*46*. 1f).

This God is unique. None can ever teach Him knowledge, from the beginning to the end (*40*. 13f; *41*. 22; etc.). There is none beside Him, and He only is Saviour (*43*. 11; *44*. 6; *45*. 5; *45*. 18; etc.). Here we find a true monotheism. There is but One God, and that God is Jehovah, the God of Israel.

2. THE TRUE ISRAEL.

Jeremiah said that those who were carried away captive in 597 B.C. were the good figs, 'very good figs, like figs that

are first ripe'. He also said that those whom the Babylonians left behind in Jerusalem were the bad figs, 'very
bad figs, which could not be eaten, they were so bad'
(Jer. *24*. 2). He followed this by saying that the captives
of Judah were taken out of Jerusalem and taken to Babylon
'for good', that is, for their ultimate prosperity. He
proclaimed that God would bring them back again into
Palestine, and would build them up and plant them in
(*24*. 5f). They will be His people, and He will be their
God, for 'they shall return to me with their whole heart'
(*24*. 7). On the other hand, those who were left behind,
Zedekiah and his nobles, and all the rest of the people
who were still in Jerusalem—all these will be scattered and
consumed. There is no future at all for them (*24*. 8–10).

Ezekiel follows in the same strain. He has nothing but
evil to say of those who were left behind in Jerusalem.
He calls them 'a rebellious house' (Ezek. *2*. 5–8; *3*. 26;
etc.). They are full of wickedness and all abominations
(*8*; *9*. 21). He too thinks of the young Jehoiachin with
favour, just as Jeremiah did. Jehoiachin is 'a tender one',
cropped off from the topmost of the young twigs, but to be
transplanted 'in the mountain of the height of Israel', to
bear fruit and to become 'a goodly cedar; and under it
shall dwell all fowl of every wing' (*17*. 22–24).

These hopes for Jehoiachin and those who went away
with him reached a partial materialisation in the closing
verses which provide the happy ending for the *Books of
Kings*. There, in 2 Kings *25*. 27–30, we read that, after
thirty years of captivity, Jehoiachin was lifted out of his
prison-house, and was given pre-eminence above all the
captive kings of Babylon.

The Second Isaiah is strong in this succession. Both
Jeremiah and Ezekiel had thought of the 597 B.C. exiles
as the nucleus of the People of God, and both of them had
extended their thought to include all the exiles, those who
went at the first and those who followed them later

(Jer. *30*; *31*. Ezek. *37*). We find the hopes of the Second Isaiah centred in the Servant of the Lord. Many scholars have identified the Servant as the Ideal Israel, a new Israel that shall emerge triumphant from all the troubles of the exile. We would agree with this, but would go farther, and would definitely identify the Servant of the Lord with the exiles of 597 B.C., those people whom already both Jeremiah and Ezekiel had declared to be the true People of God. At the same time, we find in Second Isaiah the same tendency to include all those who were deported to Babylon, both first and last.

Lastly, when we turn to the story itself of the days of the Return, those days when men in Jerusalem were trying to restore something of the former glory, we find the claim that only those who had returned from the captivity were the People of God. Their names are given in the two long lists, Ezra *2*. 1–70 and Neh. *7*. 7–73, to which should be added the list in 1 Esdras *5*. 4–46 in the *Apocrypha*. These are the men who set to work to rebuild the Temple (Ezra *2*. 68), and when 'the adversaries of Judah and Benjamin' heard that 'the children of the captivity' were busy rebuilding the Temple they came to offer help. They were refused with proud, ungenerous words: 'Ye have nothing to do with us to build an house unto our God' (Ezra *4*. 1–3). These people who were rejected were 'the people of the land', that is, the people who had never been in Babylon.

The situation, then, in the first days after the Exile, is that the exiles who came back to Jerusalem separated themselves from those whom they found in Jerusalem and its immediate environs. They claimed that they, and they alone, were the People of God, and they acted accordingly.

3. THEIR GLORIOUS DESTINY.

These exiles who came back from Babylon to Jerusalem

were supremely confident in a glorious destiny. They had known trials and anguish during their exile, and they had reached the lowest depths of despair. The prophet Ezekiel saw the wide open valley full of bones, dried and dead, the aftermath as of some great battle. The whole House of Israel was saying: 'Our bones are dried up, and our hope is lost; we are clean cut off' (37. 11). To this despairing cry the answer came firm and clear. It was that God would cause His people to come up out of their graves, and would bring them back to their own country. They would make 'an exceeding great army'.

This picture of a glowing future is found again and again in the writings of the Second Isaiah. The Servant of the Lord had certainly suffered, but the suffering belonged to the past. In referring to the well-known passage, Isa. 53, that passage which more than any other has earned the title 'suffering' for the Servant, we strictly ought not to speak of 'the suffering servant' so much as of 'the servant who has suffered'. All his suffering, now past, is regarded as preliminary to a glorious triumph. This, indeed, is the burden of the prophet's message as a whole.

The Second Isaiah is essentially the prophet of the Restoration. His message opens in chapter 40 with the statement that Jerusalem's 'warfare', her time of arduous toil and anguish, is now past. She is to be comforted; that is, there is to be an end of sorrow. There is to be a triumphant march back again over the deserts, back to Jerusalem, with every obstacle removed, 'and the glory of the Lord shall be revealed'. The message is one of good tidings to Jerusalem (40. 9–11), and all the might of the God who made heaven and earth is at work to ensure that His promises will be fulfilled. God will strengthen His chosen one (41. 8–20), and all His adversaries will be as nothing. They shall be swept away like chaff before the rising wind, and Nature herself will be transformed to make all clear for the victory of God's people. This one whom

God has raised up from the north and east will carry all before him (*41.* 25). Again and again, throughout these sixteen chapters (*40–55*), we get the same promises of a glorious future. Egypt, Ethiopia and Seba will be given as ransom for this people that they may be set free (*43.* 3), and even the mighty Babylonians will be brought low, fugitives in the day of disaster (*43.* 14ff). The produce of Egypt and Ethiopia and the trade of the Sabæans will come to the restored people (*45.* 14–17), and Israel shall never again be ashamed for ever. The idol-gods of Babylon (*46.* 1f) will be helpless in the day of their necessity, and God Himself will see to it that there will be victory in Zion, for His own glory's sake (*46.* 13).

More and more, as the message of the prophet unfolds itself, the triumph grows and spreads, till we reach the exultation of chapter *52* and of parts of chapter *54*. In this latter chapter we find the explicit expression of the belief that all the troubles of exiled Israel were but momentary and are now past. The wife who for a while was desolate and without little ones must now enlarge her tent, and only with the utmost difficulty will she be able to find accommodation for her crowding children. It was but for a small moment that she was forsaken. Only for a short while did God hide His face from her. And now that she is about to be restored His sure mercies will never leave her again. The mountains and the hills will first be moved, so enduring will be God's continued mercies to His people.

All this is nowhere more clear than in the well-known fifty-third chapter of *Isaiah*. The first nine verses tell the story of the sufferings and the exile of the Servant. He was oppressed, taken away, cut off from the land of the living, buried amongst the wealthy oppressors, and all the time without such faults as would warrant such an untimely fate. But (verses 10–12) all this is over now. When it is recognised that his suffering was undeserved, and that it was an *'asham* (translated 'an offering for sin', but it actually means in pre-Priestly Code writings, 'compensation', 'substitute') for the sins of others, then it will be realised that, when once this vicarious price has been paid, the Servant is certain to prosper and triumph. In time to come, therefore, God will see to it that the Servant takes his proper place amongst the mighty ones of the earth, for 'he shall divide the spoil with the strong'.

Such then was the teaching of the last days of the Exile. With all this in their hearts and minds the exiles came back to Jerusalem seeking to restore the ruins that had fallen down and to build them into the glorious city which the prophet had foretold. They were sure that there was One God and One God alone, mighty above all created things, unique in majesty and power, who held all nations and men in the hollow of His hand. They were sure that they were His people, they themselves and none others beside them. They were sure that for them, and for them uniquely, there was a glorious future. They were the righteous People of God, and for them even the very heavens would combine with all things earthly in bringing this great consummation to pass.

These considerations are determinative for post-exilic Judaism. Except on this basis, the whole ambition and struggle of this people are inexplicable. These hopes, and their undying certainty in respect of them, enabled them to maintain their faith in the midst of all disappointments and disasters, even to the extent of maintaining that heaven and earth would dissolve on their behalf.

CHAPTER IX

SEPARATISM

THE exiles returned from Babylon with the fixed idea that they, and they alone, were the true Israel, the People of God. We have seen, in the previous chapter, how 'the children of the captivity' refused the proffered help of 'the people of the land' (Ezra 4. 1, 4). These latter claimed to have been worshippers of Jehovah ever 'since the days of Esar-haddon, king of Assyria, which brought us up hither'. Here it is likely enough that we have some southern propaganda, which stressed the southern claim that 'the people of the land', that is, the people who were in Palestine when the exiles returned, were not true-bred Israelites, and therefore had no place at all amongst the People of God. All this is set forth in detail in 2 Kings 17. 20-41, where it is stated that Israel (i.e. the northern people) was carried away captive, 'all the seed of Israel', and that their place was taken by foreign settlers from Babylon, Cuthah, and various eastern parts of the empire, they in their turn having been deported from their homes. That there were foreign settlers brought into the country by Sargon, successor to Shalmaneser, is doubtless true. The same thing is true of the times of Esar-haddon and Asshur-bani-pal (Ezra 4. 2, 10). On the other hand, it is also true that there were many of Hebrew blood who were not deported at any time, either by Assyrian kings or by Nebuchadrezzar the Babylonian. And yet, in spite of this, the returning exiles held that every one who had not been in exile in Babylon was a foreigner, a heathen, and did not belong to the People of God.

Zerubbabel and Jeshua therefore rejected the help of these people of Palestine, some of whom might very well have been able to show as pure a descent as any who had returned from Babylon.

The returning exiles took every step possible to ensure that the exclusiveness of their claims was translated into actual practice. The genealogies (Ezra 2. 1–70. Neh. 7. 7–73. 1 Esdras 5. 4–46) formed a record to which reference could be made. Those who could prove their descent from one of the exiles mentioned in these lists thereby established their claim to be reckoned amongst the People of God.

The same separatism is to be seen in the story of the first Passover to be celebrated after the Return (Ezra 6. 19–22). The priests and the Levites purified themselves according to rule, and 'they killed the passover for all the children of the captivity, and for their brethren the priests, and for themselves'. In verse 21, however, we read that those who kept the seven days of the Feast of Unleavened Bread comprised 'the children of Israel which were come again out of the captivity, and all such as had separated themselves from the filthiness of the heathen of the land.' Evidently, therefore, the returning exiles were not able to maintain the absolute strictness which they originally sought to establish. They did admit to their company certain others who had never been in Babylon but may well have been men who could show that, even though they had continued to live in Palestine, they had never married, nor their fathers before them, a woman whose blood was not as pure as their own. On the other hand, Ezra 6. 21, may be an indication that there was a slackness, possibly even in the first days, which the more rigorous Jews sought later to counteract. Certainly by the middle of the fifth century there was considerable slackness, and that by no means on the part of the common people alone. When Nehemiah came to Jerusalem to restore the fallen fortunes of his people he met with considerable opposition.

He seems to have set about his work with a measure of secrecy from the start (Neh. *2*. 11–16). Nehemiah's opponents without the city were a Horonite (Sanballat), an Ammonite (Tobiah), and an Arabian (Geshem). But there were 'nobles of Judah' who were in constant communication with Tobiah, and 'many in Judah were sworn to him' (Neh. *6*. 17–19). Tobiah had been a thorn in the flesh of Nehemiah from the beginning. There is no especial reason for doubting the statement that he was an Ammonite, but his own good Jewish name suggests at least semi-Jewish descent. In any case, he was 'allied' to Eliashib the priest (Neh. *13*. 4), who was actually the High Priest. Tobiah was even installed in a great chamber in the Temple buildings during the period when Nehemiah had returned to the Persian court.

We have thus a picture of Nehemiah as a reformer struggling hard, against much influential opposition, to restore a separatist policy which was strong in the time of Jeshua and Zerubbabel in the first days of the Return. He fought against certain 'nobles of Judah', and against even Eliashib the High Priest himself. For not only did Eliashib support Tobiah, but one of his grandsons had married Sanballat's daughter, and Sanballat was at least as vigorous an opponent of Nehemiah as was Tobiah (Neh. *13*. 23–31).

It was small wonder, therefore, that Nehemiah's success was limited mostly to the rebuilding of the city walls. When Ezra arrived in 397 B.C. matters were in a very unsatisfactory state from the separatist point of view. As soon as Ezra arrived (Ezra *9*. 1ff), certain princes of Israel came to him and complained of those within the community who 'have not separated themselves' from the 'peoples of the lands'. Chief amongst the offenders were princes and rulers. Evidently the matter was partly political, since some of the princes and deputies were on one side and the rest were on the other.

Ezra seems to have carried the day in his own time, with the result that some time during the fourth century (the actual date is not known) the Samaritans definitely broke away from the Jerusalem Jews and built their own Temple on Mount Gerizim. We may suppose that, to whatever extent the princes and deputies were governed by political motives, the aims of Ezra were primarily religious. He was genuinely anxious to keep the People of God pure and separate from the heathen with their idolatrous associations. But there were others who were against the separatist policy, and their motives were as high and pure and genuine as any that could have influenced Ezra.

The *Book of Jonah* is one of two anti-separatist tracts which have found a place in the Old Testament. It is the story of a prophet who refused God's bidding to preach repentance to heathen Nineveh. The book belongs to the post-exilic period, as is evidenced by the somewhat late style of the Hebrew and by the way in which Nineveh has been idealised into 'an exceeding great city of three day's journey' (Jon. *3*. 3). Nineveh stands for the great oppressor, the typical tyrant city of the hostile Gentiles. She was the capital of Asshur-bani-pal, the last of the great Assyrian war-lords, the man who, until his death in 626 B.C., had for thirty-six years spread the terror of Assyria far and wide. The glee with which at least one Israelite hailed the destruction of Nineveh in 612 B.C. can be read in the *Book of Nahum*. But Jonah was commanded to go to Nineveh to preach there. He refused, and hurried with all speed to the other end of the world. God brought him back, raised a stormy wind, and made the sea rage all the more furiously when the sailors humanely tried to make a landfall in order to avoid throwing Jonah overboard. When at last Jonah was cast into the sea, forthwith an appointed large fish carried him back to land, there once more to hear the call of a God who would not be denied. This time Jonah did go to Nineveh, and he spoke the word

which was commanded him. When Nineveh repented
and was saved, Jonah was angry. He did not want to see
Nineveh saved. He wanted to see Nineveh destroyed.
In the sequel Jonah is reproved. It was right that God
should have mercy on heathen Nineveh, even on Nineveh,
that heathen city which most of all, according to the
traditions, had been the enemy of the People of God.

In this story the eighth-century prophet, Jonah the son
of Amittai (2 Kings *14*. 25) has been made to typify post-
exilic Israel, the Israel which would have nothing to do
with the heathen, separatist Israel who could say to the
'people of the land': 'Ye have nothing to do with us to
build an house to our God' (Ezra *4*. 3). The prayer of
Jonah out of the belly of the great fish is the prayer of
exiled Israel. This is to be seen in Jon. *2*. 4, and also in
verse 3, where 'the flood' and 'the waves of the sea' are
figures for the heathen (cf. Ps. *144*. 7; *93*; etc.). Yet again,
the being swallowed by a great fish is a figure used for the
Exile in Jer. *51*. 34, where the Exile is spoken of as Nebuchadrezzar devouring Israel, for 'he hath swallowed me up
like a dragon (lit. *tannin*=a sea monster)'. The book is
thus intended as a reproof to a returned separatist Israel.
It is a tract for the times, urging that the restored Israel
had a duty to the heathen, averring that the separatist
policy was contrary to the will of God.

The same emphasis is to be found in *Ruth*, an idyll of the
distant past, the story of the loves of Boaz and Ruth. Here
the story is pointed quite clearly against the separatist
policy which frowned on mixed marriages. As it has been
said, 'the sting is in the tail', in those last verses where it is
pointed out that the great-grandson of Ruth the Moabitess
was a certain David, the son of Jesse. This story, then, is
to be read against such passages as Ezra *9*, 1 ff, where it is
declared to be a dreadful thing that a true Israelite should
marry, for instance, a Moabitess. With this, compare also
Neh. *13*. 1–3 and Deut. *23*. 3–6. If then it is wrong that a

good Israelite should marry a Moabitess, how did it come about that King David himself, of all people, should be in part of Moabite ancestry, and that well within the prohibited degrees?

There is a third section of the Old Testament which is against the separatist policy. It is included in the chapters Isa. *56–66*. Nowhere is the opposition to the separatists more clear than in Isa. *56*. 1–8. Verse 3 deliberately speaks against the policy. It is wrong for any alien who has joined himself to the Lord to find himself saying, 'The Lord will surely separate me* from his people'. According to verse 6, the foreigners who join themselves to the Lord are certainly to be accepted in the Temple of the Lord, and their sacrifices accepted on the altar, 'for mine house shall be called a house of prayer for all peoples' (verse 7). Again, in Isa. *63*. 7 to *64*. 12 and in Isa. *65*. 1, we have a plea on behalf of men who have been denied access to the sanctuary. They aver that they are indeed God's people. They claim that God is indeed their father, 'though Abraham knoweth us not, and Israel doth not acknowledge us'. Meanwhile, in the intervening chapters, Isa. *57* to *63*. 6, we get passages which take the contrary and exclusive view. In these last eleven chapters, therefore, of the *Book of the Prophet Isaiah*, we get a cross-section of the opinion of the period, with its controversies and conflicting doctrines and policies. Here the strife is definitely religious. In Ezra's time there was a strong admixture of politics, but here, as in *Jonah* and *Ruth*, there is no need to suspect any other than a true religious zeal and fervour as the dominant theme. But that the intensely national stream flowed strongly can be seen in *Esther*.

There is every indication that the idea of *Habdalah* (Separation) was dominant in post-exilic days so far as the priestly circles were concerned. The idea appears again

---

* The actual Hebrew word is *habdil*; see the next and following paragraphs.

and again in the priestly tradition in the Pentateuch. Indeed this idea of Separation and Distinction is a predominant characteristic of the Priestly Code. It appears in the priestly tradition of Creation (Gen. *1–2.* 4a). In this account Creation is by Separation. The word in the English versions is 'divide', but the Hebrew root is *badal*, and it is found in the causative form, meaning 'cause a dividing, separate', i.e. in the forms *habdil, yabdil, habdel*, and so forth. The technical term *Habdalah* is from the very same root.

This principle of *Habdalah* was applied consistently in all things. God made a Separation between the holy and the profane (Lev. *10.* 10), and equally He made a Separation between Israel and the nations (Lev. *20.* 26). The priestly tradition is careful to emphasise the Separation between the clean and the unclean. This is very clear in the story of the Flood. In these chapters (Gen. *6.* 9–*9.* 17), we find two interwoven traditions, a J tradition (belonging to the south and written down about 850 B.C.) and the post-exilic P tradition. In the J story there is no distinction between clean and unclean animals (Gen. *6.* 19f). They are to be taken into the Ark 'two of every sort'. But in the P tradition, there are to be seven pairs of clean beasts and birds (Gen. *7.* 2f), but two only of unclean beasts, 'the male and his female'.

This distinction between clean and unclean is paralleled by a renewed emphasis on Holiness in the post-exilic period. The Hebrew word for 'Holiness' (*qodesh*) is a very ancient word, and it had been established as an exclusively religious word before any of the Old Testament was written.* The use, however, of the verb in its intensive (*qiddesh*) and causative (*hiqdish*) forms, in the sense

---

* For a detailed study of the meaning and development of the word, see A. B. DAVIDSON: *Theology of the Old Testament* (1904), pp. 114–157, 252–259. See also my *The Distinctive Ideas of the Old Testament* (1944), pp. 21–54.

of 'set apart', is largely a product of late-exilic and post-exilic times. It belongs to the time when separatist ideas were becoming more and more a dominant factor in Jewish thought and practice. The development and the increased emphasis is to be seen in the 'Holiness (H)' section of *Leviticus* (*17–26*), in the Priestly Code proper, and in the writings of the Chronicler, that is, in *Ezra, Nehemiah, 1* and *2 Chronicles*, those writings which form the post-exilic history of the world out of which the Jews were separated.

SABBATH.

The separatist tendency is to be seen in the post-exilic development of the Sabbath. Increased importance was given to the observance of this day during the formative period of Judaism which belongs to the early post-exilic period. This is to be seen in Isa. *56.* 2 and 6, where the keeping of the Sabbath is in each case the first and presumably most important item in the list. It has become of the utmost importance to 'sanctify (*hiqdish*) the Sabbath day' (Neh. *13.* 22), i.e. to separate it from the others. In Neh. *13.* 18 the non-observance of the Sabbath in pre-exilic times is specially cited as a cause of the calamities of that time. This may mean that Nehemiah, at any rate, or possibly the editors, believed that there was something wrong from their point of view in the way in which the Sabbath was observed in pre-exilic times.

We know that in pre-exilic times the Sabbath was known as a day distinct from the ordinary work-day. This is clear from such a passage as Amos *8.* 5. But there it is equated with the new-month-day as a day on which corn cannot be sold. Similarly, in 2 Kings *4.* 23, the new-month-day and the Sabbath are days when the gentleman-farmer's wife might expect to have one of the young men and one of the she-asses for a journey to see the man of God. It is evident that here the Sabbath was not hedged about with the taboos of later times. These taboos had their origin in the taboos which were associated with the new-month-days and the 'seven'-days in the old Assyrian calendars. In the time of Asshur-bani-pal all the taboo days were abolished except the 'seven'-days, and observance of the latter was the rule during Babylon's time of prosperity, when the Jews were in exile there. There is good ground for believing that here we have the origin of the new restrictions as to the length of the journey that might be undertaken on the Sabbath, and of the limitations of the work of the physician, and so forth.* But the Jews took these special restrictions, and turned them into special observances which marked the Jew off from the Gentiles. The taboos became separatist rites, a development which was made all the easier with the collapse of Mesopotamian customs before the Persian Zoroastrian culture.

When the strict observance of the Sabbath rules became a primary test of faithfulness to the Law, it became necessary for all the details to be worked out with the utmost care and exactitude. This was done steadily during the next three centuries or so, and in this way there grew up a great body of oral tradition, much of which was finally written down in the *Mishnah*.† The regulations for the Sabbath are to be found in the Mishnah tract *Shabbat*, wherein every kind of action is discussed in relation to the Sabbath taboos. The things which were permitted to be done were stripped down to the barest necessity, and every kind of nicety of judgement came to be involved.

In respect of the 'traditions of the elders' there is this much to be said. If it be held that a man can merit entrance into the Kingdom of Heaven by his strict observance of the Law, then obviously his wisdom is to see to it that the experts should work out for him the way in which

---

* For details see my *The Jewish New Year Festival* (1947), pp. 106ff.

† There is an excellent translation of *The Mishnah* by Professor H. Danby (1933).

the Law is to be applied to the smallest details of daily
life. This is what the scribes did, and the more accurately
they worked out the implications of the Law, the more
faithful they were to their high calling. Their position is
sound and logical, given their premise. In practice such
casuistry, however sanctified and well-intentioned, has its
peril; and the peril is that a man might come not to be able
to see the wood for the trees. Or to use the famous
picture-phrase of the Lord Jesus, he might strain out
gnats whilst he swallowed down whole camels. The
tendency was to 'tithe mint and anise and cummin', and to
leave 'undone the weightier matters of the law, judgement,
and mercy, and faith' (Matt. *23*. 23f). Or again, if, as
St. Paul held, salvation is by faith and not by works, that
is, if entrance into the Kingdom of Heaven depends upon
an attitude of humble trust in God, and not on the actions
a man has done, then the whole system falls to the ground.
But, given their premise, their position was sound.

CIRCUMCISION.

A similar change took place in connection with the rite
of circumcision. There is no doubt that this rite was always
practised by the Hebrews, as their very early designation
of their western neighbours as 'uncircumcised Philistines'
shows. The Philistines were, in fact, the only people
known to the Hebrews who did not practise the rite. It
was the custom in Egypt and amongst the surrounding
peoples also. We know now that the rite has been wide-
spread amongst primitive peoples the whole world round.
The difference which the exile made was that circumcision
became a mark in the flesh which separated the Jew off
from other peoples. It was a sign in the body of that
unique covenant which existed between Jehovah and His
chosen people. This is clear from the Priestly Code
account of the circumcision of Abraham in Gen. *17*. 1-14.
Who so remains uncircumcised is cut off from the People

of God. But all this is post-exilic. There is no reference to circumcision in the earlier laws, and the rite is nowhere enjoined, before the time of the Priestly Code, as having any particular significance. The early reference is the curious story of Exod. *4.* 26 (J), and the circumcision by Joshua in Josh. *5.* 2–9 (J and D).

Originally it was a puberty rite, definitely connected with fitness for marriage, as in Exod. *4.* 26; but it came to be the mark of the People of God, made in the flesh as soon as the seventh day of the birth period was past. This is a particular development amongst the Hebrews, whereby a puberty rite of admission to the tribe becomes an infant rite of admission into the People of God. It can be paralleled by the way in which Baptism has developed into infant sprinkling amongst some Christians. In each case the rite has become less severe with its transference to infancy.

All this is evidence which mostly relates to the earlier period of the Persian rule, down to the early years of Artaxerxes II (Mnemon), who began to reign in 404 B.C. But the same sort of thing existed in the later Persian period, and in the earlier part of the Greek period also. Hecatæus of Abdera (306–283 B.C.), said that 'under the later rule of the Persians and of the Macedonians, who overthrew the empire of the latter, many of the traditional customs of the Jews were altered owing to their intercourse with aliens'.

We have seen that from the times of Zerubbabel and Jeshua there was a considerable body of opposition to the dominant separatist policy, whether on political grounds or on religious grounds. These divisions of opinion and policy are equally in evidence in the times of Nehemiah and Ezra, and all through the fourth century B.C. also. Matters came to a head in the second century in the time of Antiochus IV (Epiphanes, 175–163 B.C.). The evidence is to be found in the *Books of the Maccabees*, particularly in

F

the first book, which historically is by far the more reliable.

In the time of Antiochus IV 'came there forth out of Israel transgressors of the Law, and persuaded many, saying, Let us go and make a covenant with the Gentiles that are round about us . . .' (1 Macc. *1.* 11). We then read how 'certain of the people were forward' in this matter. They went to the king and he gave them permission 'to do after the ordinances of the Gentiles'. In particular, a gymnasium was built in Jerusalem after the Greek custom, and young Jews sought to imitate the Greeks in their athletic exercises. Incidentally, they had to run naked in public, to the great offence of the orthodox. Especially they 'made themselves uncircumcised, and forsook the holy covenant, and joined themselves to the Gentiles' (1 Macc. *1.* 15). There came a time, in the days of the Bar-Kokheba revolt in the second century A.D. (in the time of Hadrian), when the custom developed of tearing the flesh with the thumbnail in addition to cutting the foreskin with a knife, in order to prevent this operation which would hide an earlier circumcision. We can see, in the case of both rebellions, both that of Judas Maccabæus and Bar-Kokheba, that the matter of circumcision takes on increased importance when the Law is challenged. After Mattathias and his friends had fled to the mountains they went from place to place, pulling down the heathen altars which the Greek officers had established, 'and they circumcised by force the children that were uncircumcised, as many as they found in the coasts of Israel' (1 Macc. *2.* 46).

It is evident that Antiochus IV was by no means in the position of trying to force Gentile ways on a wholly separatist people. He had many friends inside the country, men who were in favour, for whatever reason, of coming to reasonable terms with the foreigner. It was only after the incident at Modein, when the aged Mattathias slew the Greek officer and fled to the hills, that the separatists began to gather together to take common action. The movement grew under Judas, the third of the sons of Mattathias, till at last he was joined by the Chasidim, those who were zealous for the Law from a strictly religious point of view. Then it was that these separatists became dominant, for the Chasidim fought with fanatical zeal.

But here again it is difficult to say where politics ended and religion began. There is no doubt about the attitude of the Chasidim. Their sole interest was in religion, and it was for the preservation and establishment of the Law that they fought. As soon as this was achieved, and Judas began to fight on for political freedom, the Chasidim began to leave him. That, as much as anything else, provides the explanation of Judas's failure at Elasa because of the very small force which fought with him.

We have seen that the princes and deputies who supported Ezra were most probably moved by political considerations rather than by religious ideals. The behaviour of the Hasmonæan princes often leaves yet more to be desired. Many of them were by no means averse to a participation in the delights that the Greek way of life offered. That there was a clash between the two ways of life is certain. Zech. 9. 13 is evidence of this: 'And I will stir up thy sons, O Zion, against thy sons, O Greece.' Some scholars allege that this is an interpolation, but if so, it is earlier than the translation of the Old Testament into Greek (the *Septuagint*). The Jews in Jerome's time (*c*. A.D. 400) saw in it a reference to the times of the Maccabees, and Rashi (A.D. 1040–1105) also refers to the Hasmonæans (the successors of the Maccabees). It is probable that the passage is rather earlier, but whatever the period, it indicates the struggle of the two ideologies.

There came to be a curious change-over. Whereas, judging from the Priestly Code, it was the priests who were at first most zealous in the separatist movement, the time came when the wealthy priestly aristocracy were zealous chiefly in maintaining friendly relations with the ruling power. They are not the first men of any calling, their own or another, whom power and money and influence have corrupted, and it is more than probable that their race is not yet dead. The mantle of the separatists who would keep Jewry pure and unspotted from the devices of the heathen fell upon such groups as the Chasidim, of whom the Pharisees were in part the descendants. By the first century A.D., it was the Pharisees who were the custodians of the Law, and the Sadducees who were less enthusiastic. For almost a hundred years, from the time of Alexandra Salome (75–74 B.C.), the Pharisees had been the upholders of religious duties in so far as the Oral Law was concerned on the one hand, and, on the other, of correct procedure in the religious rites in the Temple itself.

The separatist movement can be illustrated from Jewish books other than the *Books of the Maccabees*. The prohibition against intermarriage with the heathen is to be found in the *Book of Tobit*, written probably towards the close of the third century B.C. 'And take first a wife of the seed of thy fathers, and take not a strange wife which is not of thy father's tribe: for we are all sons of the prophets' (*4*. 12). The same prohibition is found also in *The Testaments of the Twelve Patriarchs* (Levi *9*. 10): 'Take, therefore, to thyself a wife without blemish or pollution, while yet thou art young, and not of the race of strange nations.' The passage belongs to the latter half of the second century B.C., the time of John Hyrcanus. The *Book of Jubilees*, belonging to the same period, is very strong for separatism, doubtless because of the powerful Hellenising forces at work in Palestine during the period when the Hasmonæans were kings as well as priests. Marriages with Gentiles are strictly prohibited in this book (*20*. 4; *22*. 20; *25*. 1–10), especially in *30*. 1–17, where death by stoning is prescribed for any Israelite who would give his daughter or sister to a Gentile, and the woman is to be burned to death. There is no evidence that any rules like this were ever put into force, but the passage shows the kind of propaganda which the separatists were putting out during that period. They believed it to be 'abominable before the Lord' for any Jew to give his daughter to a Gentile, or to take a Gentile woman for his son.

There are other passages which prohibit any mingling with the Gentiles, e.g. 2 Macc. *11*. 24; *14*. 3; Psalms of Solomon *17*. 30 f, which reads 'for He knoweth them (i.e. the Jews) that they are all the children of God, and He shall divide them according to their tribes upon the earth: and the sojourner and the foreigner shall not dwell with them'. Or again, the attitude of the first century A.D. is to be seen in 2 (4) Esdras *6*. 56–59, where the well-known passage in Isa. *40*. 15–17 receives a new and characteristic interpretation. The prophet intended, it is generally agreed, to say that all peoples of earth, i.e. all human kind, are as nothing before God, and are reckoned as a drop from a bucket. But this first century author makes these verses refer to the other nations which are descended from Adam, and not to the Jews at all. The heathen are the peoples which are as nothing and like spittle, and like a drop falling from a bucket; whereas the world was created for the sake of Israel.

It would, however, be an error to assume that such a separatism, with all its pride of race, was characteristic of post-exilic Jewry as a whole. There were indeed many who were willing to countenance mingling with the Gentiles from unworthy motives, but there were also those who were willing, and even eager, to welcome any Gentile who was prepared to fulfil the conditions imposed by the Law. There were two streams of thought from the Exile onwards. On the one hand, there was the stream which would have nothing to do with the Gentiles on any account, sometimes from exclusively national motives and on the basis of a

rigid pure-blood theory, but sometimes from genuinely
religious motives, believing that such contact would weaken
and in time destroy Judaism. On the other hand, there
was the stream which was anxious to extend the blessings
of the true religion to whoever was willing to accept the
conditions. This is the attitude of the anti-separatist
tracts, *Jonah* and *Ruth*. It is put forward at its best in
Isa. *56.* 6f, and in other similar passages, by Third-
Isaiah. Ben-Sira admits no distinction between Jew and
Gentile as such. According to the Hebrew version of
Ecclus. *10.* 22 he wrote, 'sojourner and stranger, foreigner
and poor man, their glorying is in the fear of the Lord'.
This is the general attitude in the *Testaments of the Twelve
Patriarchs*, even in the first century B.C. additions. For
instance, there is the passage which has been interpolated
into Test. Judah *24.* 5, 6, where the writer speaks of a stem
which shall arise out of Jacob, from which 'shall grow a
rod of righteousness to the Gentile, to judge and save all
that call upon the Lord'. Or again in Test. Benjamin
9. 2 (late second century B.C.) where all the Gentiles are
to be gathered together equally with the twelve tribes to
the last Temple (more glorious than the first) 'until the
Most High shall send forth His salvation in the visitation
of the only-begotten prophet'. This attitude is general
in the *Testaments*, e.g. Levi *2.* 11 ; *4.* 4 ; *8.* 14. Simeon *6.* 5.
Naphtali *8.* 3. Asher *7.* 3. Dan *6.* 7. Judah *25.* 5.
Benjamin *9.* 4.

Generally, however, writings which originated in
Palestine during the last three centuries of the pre-
Christian era are dominated by the separatist *motif*, and
this is true of the first century A.D. also. On the other hand,
writings which originated from outside Palestine are wider
in their sympathies. These are the work of the Jews of
the Dispersion, whose contact with the Gentiles had
brought them to a less separatist frame of mind, men who
had perforce to arrive at a working compromise with the

Gentile world in which they lived. One aspect of this is to be seen in the frequent reference in the *Acts of the Apostles* to 'devout' persons in connection with the synagogues of Asia Minor and Greece. These were Gentiles who worshipped the God of the Jews but were uncircumcised, and probably did not follow the food rules. Amongst them were the 'devout Greeks' at Thessalonica (*17.* 4), and there is also reference to 'devout women of honourable estate' at Antioch in Pisidia (*13.* 50). These were not proselytes who did fully accept the conditions of Judaism.

One of the foremost Jews of the Dispersion was Philo of Alexandria, who flourished in the first half of the first century A.D. He was firm for the Jewish Law in respect of the Sabbath and circumcision, but was most anxious to commend the tenets of Judaism to the Gentiles. With him proselytes stand on an equal footing with those who are Jews by birth. He holds that Moses himself commanded the Israelites to love their Gentile converts as themselves. He definitely rebuts the charges of exclusiveness on the ground of Judaism's willingness to receive proselytes, and makes a great deal of the fact that Abraham, the ancestor of the Jews, was by birth a Chaldæan. Abraham, in fact, is the pattern for all proselytes, for he gave up inhuman customs and eschewed idol worship in order to turn to the life which truth watches and guards.

After the rebellion in the time of Hadrian we find a less exclusive attitude in Palestine also. This appears amongst the third generation of Tannaim (teachers of the *Mishnah*), who flourished about the middle of the second century A.D., though in the first century we have the famous Hillel, whose sympathies were notably warm and generous to all men.

CHAPTER X

THE GLORIOUS FUTURE

WE have seen that, thanks to the rich promises of the Second Isaiah, the Jews who returned from the Babylonian Exile looked forward to a glorious future, when all the sorrows of the Exile would be forgotten in joy and prosperity. The story of post-exilic Jewry is the story of dreams that faded one after the other, dreams that never materialised except in fitful promise. This was the history of three and a half centuries without intermission. There came the short-lived success of Judas Maccabæus, soon to be eclipsed by his death in 160 B.C. at Elasa. We get a temporary lifting of the cloud in the time of Simon, the last of the five sons of Mattathias, but even the great John Hyrcanus was in a most precarious plight until the death of Antiochus VII (Sidetes) in 129 B.C. Then indeed for a generation the flower of Jewish nationalist hopes blossomed and grew to full power. No sooner, however, had Hyrcanus established himself and extended his power than internal strife began to weaken the nation. This internal strife increased with the years, so that the conquests of Alexander Jannæus, great as they were, marched parallel with bloodshed and bitterness at home. The strife continued; faction fights weakened the unity of the people, and with each party appealing for foreign help against the other the glory of Jewry faded. Not of this world was the promised glory to come.

The hope of a glorious future was by no means confined to the post-exilic period. Such a hope is indeed characteristic of all peoples at all stages of their development.

Usually it takes the form, though with varying degress of
approximation, of a hope of return to an original state of
happiness, an idealised past, since when things have gone
steadily from bad to worse.   The general hope of mankind
is that the New Year will see a change of fortune for the
better.   Certainly amongst the Hebrews this was the case,
for in pre-exilic times the change of fortune was connected
with the first day of the great autumnal feast, the Feast of
Ingathering which marked the close of the agricultural
year.   This was the 'Day of the Lord', and it came at
the end of the harvest when the late summer was past.
Jeremiah speaks of the disappointment which one particular
'Day of the Lord' brought, when he cried: 'The harvest
is past, the summer (*qayits*, properly the late summer, a
time of intense heat) is ended, and we are not saved'
(Jer. *8*. 20).

Out of the general hope of a better fortune at the turn
of the year there arose the hope of a specially great Day
of the Lord when the fallen fortunes of Israel would be
established firmly for ever.   This idea was already established in the time of Amos, for he makes it his business to
disabuse the minds of Israel of their easy optimism.   They
expected that the Day of the Lord would necessarily be
for them a day of light.   They looked forward to it with
anticipation and longing.   Amos cries: 'Woe to you that
desire (better, 'long for') the Day of the Lord.   Wherefore
indeed would ye have the Day of the Lord?   It is darkness
and not light' (*5*. 18).   He goes on to say that when this
Day of the Lord comes, this day which they hope will
bring security for them from their ills, it will be 'out of the
frying pan into the fire'.   A man flees from a lion, only
to fall into the clutch of a bear.   He dashes breathless into
his house and leans his hand against the wall, as he thank-
fully recovers his breath, only to find that a snake has
bitten him.   'Shall not the Day of the Lord be darkness,
and not light?   Even gross darkness with no brightness in

it?' (verse 20). And so, in the mind of the pre-exilic prophet, Amos, the Day of the Lord is by no means a day of joy.

We find the same picture in Isa. 2. 6-21, with its refrain in verses 11 and 17: 'and the loftiness of man shall be bowed down, and the haughtiness of men shall be brought low: and the Lord alone shall be exalted in that day', or again, in verse 12, 'for the Lord of Hosts hath a day (*R.V. margin*) against all that is proud and haughty and upon all that is lifted up'.

The Day of the Lord, therefore, comes to be a day for the exaltation of God alone. None but the righteous who do His will can hope to stand in that day. It will be a day of doom and darkness for all evil and so for all evil men. Amos sees little hope of any relief in the oncoming gloom. The fate of Israel, the northern kingdom, is that she will go into captivity beyond Damascus, and carry with her her images of the star-god she has worshipped, Sakkut, the Assyrian god Nidib, whose star was the planet Saturn-Kewan (5. 26f). Hosea knows that Israel, his own people, must suffer punishment, but he does look forward to a better day when the tribulation is over, a day when Israel will be betrothed to God in faithfulness, and when a new fertility will bring prosperity of corn and oil and wine (2. 20ff). Isaiah has much to say in condemnation of all the wicked, wherever they are found. He has no hope of Ephraim the northern kingdom, any more than Amos, the other southerner, had. But here again his love for his own people causes him to look forward to the advent of a scion of David's line, 'a shoot out of the stock of Jesse' (*11.* 1), under whose wise and God-guided rule righteousness and faithfulness to God shall spread through the land. A new era of peace shall be established which shall include even the mutual enemies of the natural world, 'for the earth shall be full of the knowledge of the Lord, as the waters cover the sea' (*11.* 1-9).

With Jeremiah, as we have seen, we get a clarification of the issue which is of the utmost importance for the future. He, too, is full of condemnation, but as the years pass by his condemnation is reserved for those who remained behind in Jerusalem after the 597 B.C. deportation. These are the 'bad figs', whereas the exiles of 597 B.C. are the 'good figs'. To these, 'the captives of Judah', God will 'give . . . an heart to know me, that I am the Lord: and they shall be my people, and I will be their God: for they shall return unto me with their whole heart' (24. 7). This estimation of exiled Israel as righteous is carried on into the writings of the Second Isaiah and of Ezekiel. The result is that post-exilic Israel, being now conscious of its righteousness, can once more look forward with hope to the Day of the Lord.

Post-exilic expectation is therefore once more full of those glowing hopes which belonged to popular thought in the eighth century, when Amos and his contemporaries were active. 'The wilderness and the solitary place shall be glad; and the desert shall rejoice, and blossom as the rose. . . . They shall see the glory of the Lord, the excellency of our God' (Isa. 35. 1f). Under the influence of this new confidence interpolations find their way into the writing of the earlier prophets, since their wholesale condemnations now need qualification. Such interpolations are to be found in Hos. 1. 10, 11. Amos 9. 5–15. Isa. 30. 19–26. The time will be one of great contentment. The idyllic picture of peaceful security is that 'they shall sit every man under his own vine and under his fig-tree; and none shall make them afraid' (Mic. 4. 4. 1 Kings 4. 25. Zech. 3. 10. 1 Macc. 14. 12). In those days righteousness will flourish and all the righteous shall partake of the glorious bliss.

It has been supposed that the idea of the advent of good fortune at the turn of the year in connection with the great autumnal feast is due mostly to the influence of Babylonian

religion.   We know that during the period when the Jews
were domiciled in Babylon there was an annual festival
observed in the autumn with the most elaborate ceremony.
Every year the idol-gods of Babylonia were brought in
procession into the Great Hall of Marduk at Babylon, and
there they 'fixed the fates' for the coming year.   They did
this on two distinct occasions, on the eighth day and again
on the eleventh day, and Nebo, the scribe of the gods,
wrote down on the tablets of destiny the fates, both good
and bad, which the gods had decreed.   This double fixing
of the fate of the coming year is a strange procedure, and
all the more so because there is a double fixing of the fate
in the great Creation Epic which was recited at the festival.
There were other rites, namely the ritual marriage of the
god, an acted drama in which the god is killed to rise again,
and a triumphal procession.   The view has been strongly
advocated during the last twenty years that the Jews were
greatly influenced by such rites, and that there were substantial elements in their pre-exilic cultus, surviving to some
degree in the post-exilic cultus, of this original myth-ritual
pattern, alleged to be common to the whole of the Near
East.   Opinion is now turning away somewhat from these
urbanised rites towards an agricultural variant such as is
to be found portrayed in the finds at Ugarit, near to the
mouth of the Orontes in northern Syria.   In any case,
there is no need to assume a Babylonian exilic origin for
the idea of fixing the fate at the turn of the year.   Such
ideas are common to all peoples the whole world over.

THE DEVELOPMENT OF THE IMAGERY.

Thanks to Amos, the Day of the Lord became in Jewish
thought a Day of Judgement for all evil, and a Day of
Victory for the righteous God.   We have seen how, after
the exile, the victory of the righteous God became a victory
for the restored and righteous Israel.   The Day of the
Lord remains a Day of Judgement for all that is alien to

God, and by contrast comes more and more to be a Day
of Judgement for the heathen world. As a Day of Judgement, it is a day of darkness. In a very curious way the
imagery of the Day of the Lord grows from prophet to
prophet, and chief in the development is the detailed
intensification of the darkness.

In Zeph. *1*. 7–18 we have a late seventh-century
description of the Day of the Lord. Zephaniah was an
early contemporary of the prophet Jeremiah, and it is
probable that his teaching was concerned with the threat
of the Scythians in the year 627 B.C., when they swept
through the Cilician Gates into Syria and down the coast-
lands. In this oracle the darkness of Amos has become
darker still. 'That day is a day of wrath, a day of trouble
and distress, a day of wasteness and desolation, a day of
darkness and gloominess, a day of clouds and thick darkness' (Zeph. *1*. 15).

About a hundred years later, but earlier than the rise
of Cyrus, we find another picture of judgement upon the
wicked. Here, in Isa. *13*, the prophet is looking forward
to the destruction of Babylon. He is envisaging a hoped-
for attack of the Medes on Babylon, when scenes of great
brutality and ruthless savagery will take place (verses
15–16). This is the day of the Lord's fierce anger. It
will come 'cruel, with wrath and fierce anger . . . for the
stars of heaven and the constellations thereof shall not
give their light; the sun shall be darkened in his going
forth, and the moon shall not cause her light to shine'
(*13*. 9, 10). Here the portrayal is more detailed than
ever, and in verse 13 a new element is added to the
picture : 'I will make the heavens to tremble, and the earth
shall be shaken out of her place' before the terrifying anger
of the Lord.

We come next to *Joel*, later by perhaps another century.
Here, in Joel *2*. 2, we find the 'day of darkness and gloominess, a day of clouds and thick darkness' of Zeph. *1*. 15.

We find also the trembling heavens and the quaking earth of Isa. *13*. 13. But there is a more lurid picture than ever of 'wonders in the heavens and the earth, blood, and fire, and pillars of smoke. The sun shall be turned into darkness (i.e. eclipsed), and the moon into blood (also eclipsed, the reference being to the curious copper colour of the eclipsed moon), before the great and terrible day of the Lord come' (*2*. 30f).

And so the terrors of the Day of the Lord increase, darker and yet more dark, full of a growing terror and fear. All this is the work of the prophets, each man drawing in the colours and the lines more and more faithfully and emphasising the fierce anger of the Lord against evil, together with the awful terror which will herald His approach. The full picture is to be seen in the first century A.D. *Assumption of Moses*: 'For the Heavenly One shall arise from the throne of His kingdom, and shall come out of His holy habitation with indignation and wrath for His children. And the earth shall quake: even to its bounds shall it be shaken: and the lofty mountains shall be brought low and shall be shaken, and the valleys shall fall. The sun shall not give his light, and the horns of the moon shall be turned into darkness, and they shall be broken, and the whole of the moon shall be turned into blood. And the circuit of the stars shall be disordered; and the sea shall fall even to the abyss: the fountains of water shall fail, and the rivers be afraid' (*10*. 3–6). Compare the picture in Matt. *24*. 29. An extraordinary, still fuller, expansion is to be found in Sibylline Oracles, *5*. 512–530, where we have a detailed description of war amongst the constellations, with especial confusion in the Zodiac.

THE APOCALYPSES.

To this terrible picture of the event which will mark the end of the reign of evil there was added during the centuries a conception which came through Persian Zoroastrianism.

It is possible that the idyllic picture of the Garden of Eden gathered something from the old Zoroastrian story of the garden of Yima, the good shepherd king who ruled in the golden age when all was good and fair, Yima the gloriously resplendent man, perfect and upright in body and mind. In that golden time there was no death, and no old age, nor any cold or heat, in the wonderful garden that was set on the mysterious mountain in the north. The story of the Garden of Eden in *Genesis* has traces of this ancient myth of the Garden of God, notably in the four streams which flowed out from it, and there is other evidence in the picture of Eden in Ezek. *28.* 13ff, with its avenue of jewel-bearing trees, and again in the miraculous tree of Ezek. *31.* But the greatest Zoroastrian influence is to be found in the conception of successive ages of the world.

The Persian (Iranian) conception of the whole scheme of things envisages four world-periods, or ages, each of three thousand years in duration. In the first Age the creation was entirely spiritual and invisible. From before the beginning there were two spirits, Ahura Mazda, the good spirit, and Angra Mainyu, the evil spirit. When Angra Mainyu saw the light of this first creation he sought by every means to defeat the good spirit, Ahura Mazda. All the efforts which he made were unavailing during the second Age of three thousand years. They were years of blessedness, a veritable Golden Age. But in the third period of three thousand years the evil spirit gained an ascendancy and created every kind of evil thing, including a hundred thousand diseases, save one. At the end of this period of three thousand years Zarathushtra (in the Greek Zoroaster) appears and the victory of Ahura Mazda begins. At the end of each thousand years a deliverer (Shaoshyant) appears, born of the line of Zarathushtra, though earlier traditions suggest that this Shaoshyant is always Zarathushtra himself. At last there comes the great consummation when Angra Mainyu (Ahriman) is cast into the abyss by Ahura Mazda (Ormuzd), and the end of the world takes place. Then the dead will be raised and all men will be judged. Fire will descend from heaven and all things will be burned. All men will pass through this purifying fire, but finally all will be saved, and a new Age will begin, with new heavens and a new earth. All will be happiness, and there will be no evil, nor pain, nor sorrow.

During all these centuries the Jews were looking for a glorious Age that never came. Time and again they hoped that some change in the balance of power would give them the opportunity to fulfil the glorious destiny which they believed to be theirs as the People of God. But that opportunity never came, and generation after generation passed. At last the Jews began to realise that if ever a glorious destiny was to come for them it could never arise out of the ordinary course of the world's history. It would have to come directly from God Himself. The Iranian eschatology (i.e. doctrine of 'the last things') sketched above provided a solution for a people who were being slowly driven to the realisation that this present world held nothing for them but blood and tears and humiliation. The Iranian doctrine told them that this Age was indeed the Age when wickedness triumphed and the power of evil was supreme. But it told them also that when this Age was past, then the New Age would begin. Then, in that time, the People of God would realise those blessings which had so long been denied to them.

The first influence of Iranian eschatology is to be found in the early apocalypse Isa. *24–27*. This dates from the third century B.C., the time of the rivalries of the Ptolemies and the Seleucids. Some authorities would place the section as late as 200 B.C. It speaks of the emptying and the spilling out of the inhabitants of a world turned upside down (*24.* 1), to be followed by a burning of them all so that only a few are left (*24.* 6). The judgement was against 'the high ones on high' (*24. 21*), and they, together with the kings of earth, those who have exercised dominion over. their subjects, including the Jews, will be cast into the pit and there punished. Here, too, in this section we have a resurrection of the Jews (*26. 19*), though their adversaries have been destroyed by fire (*26. 11*), and shall not live again. This is far from the full eschatological scheme of the new heavens and the new earth, but there is enough of the imagery to show that the Iranian scheme is known.

Once again, this time in Isa. *65. 17*, we find indications of an acquaintance with the Iranian scheme of Creation. The prophet, perhaps in the fifth century B.C. (though these verses may well be considerably later than other sections in these last eleven chapters), speaks in terms of 'new heavens and a new earth'. It will be a time of rejoicing, for there shall be no more sorrow (verse 19). Men will live to such a great age that even a centenarian will be regarded as an infant. Everywhere, amongst both man and beast, there will be peace and blessedness. This again falls short of the full scheme, but there are traces of Iranian influence.

The second century B.C. saw a great revival of Jewish hopes, and with it an increased use of phraseology from Iranian eschatology in the descriptions of them. Especially was this the case when Judas Maccabæus was gaining his successes against the Syrian-Greek forces, and was able to restore the Temple worship in December, 164 B.C. This great event is commemorated in the Festival of Chanukkah (Dedication). O. S. Rankin has shown* that this displaced the Syrian New Year festival and took over many of its New Age rites. The connection with Iranian eschatology can be seen in the *Book of Daniel*. In chapter 7 we have a picture of God Himself in the likeness of a very old man ('ancient of days') seated on His throne in the midst of fiery flames, with a fiery stream issuing forth before

---

* *The Origins of the Festival of Hanukkah* (1930), pp. 203f.

G

Him (7. 9f). Then was the beast (i.e. the great enemy of God) slain and his body burned with fire (7. 11), with the result that, the enemy of God having been defeated, the kingdom of the saints (verses 13f, 22f) shall never pass away. Once more, when the time is fulfilled, we read of a resurrection (12. 2), and a purifying and a living for ever and ever (12. 10, 3). The restoration of the worship in December, 164 B.C., was thus visualised as the End of the Time, the three and a half years of the *Book of Daniel*. The New Age had begun.

With the close of the century the glory of the Hasmonæans passed, and with this began a spate of books almost wholly given over to the imagery of Iranian eschatology. It is probable that in the two Isaianic passages to which reference has been made (*24-27* and *65*. 17, etc.) the imagery of the Iranians has been used without any particular thought of its actual literal fulfilment, and this, too, may well be the case in the *Book of Daniel*. But the following century is the period of the apocalypses, those books which tell of that which is shortly to come to pass. In these writings more and more a literal fulfilment is expected. They are invariably pseudonymous, written in the name of some ancient character long since dead. They purport to contain secrets long hidden, but now revealed for the edification and salvation of those who are living in the last days. Everything is both vivid and urgent. The time of the great consummation is near, knocking at the doors. There is scarcely one eminent figure of ancient days whose name is not pressed into service. In the Old Testament we have the name of Daniel, for parts of the book which is found under his name form the first true apocalypse. During the last two centuries B.C. appeared the *Book of Jubilees*, which is in the form of revelations granted to Moses at Sinai, and on that account has been called 'the little Genesis'; the *Testaments of the Twelve Patriarchs*, that is, of the twelve sons of Jacob; and the

Book of Enoch, in many respects the most famous and the most important of them all. In the first century A.D., there is an overflow of such writings. The names used are Moses, Abraham, Enoch again, Adam and Eve, Ezra, Baruch, Isaiah, and, in the New Testament, John the Divine.* It is indeed most important in the study of these writings to realise that the writers are speaking of events of the immediate future, 'the things which must shortly come to pass' (Rev. *1*. 1). See also II Esdras *9*. 1–13.

We have already seen that, apart altogether from Iranian influence, the Day of the Lord has become a day of judgement, heralded by darkness and terror, with sun, moon and stars eclipsed, and heaven and earth quaking and being shaken out of their place. Now the Iranian eschatology with its lurid picture of the End of the Last Age adds its terrors of destruction by fire to the already dreadful picture. This destroying river of fire appears, as we have seen, in Dan. *7*. 10. It is to be found in Enoch *17*. 1, 4, 5; in the Psalms of Solomon *15*. 6f; in the Sibylline Oracles *3*. 54; II Esdras *5*. 8; 2 Baruch *27*. 10; *70*. 8; and, in the New Testament, in 2 Pet. *3*. 10; 1 Cor. *3*. 15; and frequently in *Revelation*.

The apocalypses envisage judgement upon the heathen and they are full of terrible pictures of the fate of the wicked. On the other hand, they contain most fulsome descriptions of the blessings of the Age to Come. When all the terrors of the End of the Age have passed, then on a new earth and under new heavens the glorious destiny of the People of God will be realised. Already there had been something of this in the writings of the Second Isaiah, with his pictures

---

* For a description and discussion of these apocalypses, see H. H. ROWLEY: *The Relevance of Apocalyptic* (1944); C. C. TORREY: *The Apocryphal Literature* (1945), which is somewhat wider in its scope. The English texts of most of these writings have been published by the S.P.C.K. in the series *Translations of Early Documents*. The Ezra-apocalypse is to be found in the *Apocrypha*, where it comprises II Esdras (in the Vulgate, 4 Ezra) *3–14*.

of the transformation of Nature, beginning .with *40*. 3f, and continuing with such passages as *41*. 18f; *44*. 23; *51*. 3; *55*. 12f; and in *35*, which belongs to the same type of thought.   An early picture of the bliss of the New Age is to be found in Isa. *45*. 19–25; and other descriptions are to be found in Sibylline Oracles *3*. 744ff.   Enoch *10*. 16–*11*. 11.   2 Baruch *51*. 7–16.   II Esdras *7*. 88–98; *8*. 52. Rev. *21–22*. 5.

THE DATE OF THE END OF DAYS.

Another feature of apocalyptic literature is the attempt to fix the date of the End of Days.   Here there is a double strand, one which seems to be Jewish in origin, and the other Iranian.

The attempts to fix the time of the Last Day along the line of Jewish tradition arise out of the 'seventy years' of Jer. *29*. 10.   The prophet Jeremiah is advising the exiles to settle down in Babylon, in the land of their captivity. Apparently there have been prophets amongst the exiles, diviners who have told the people that they will very soon return to their homeland.   Jeremiah holds out no such hope, but bids the people reconcile themselves to a prolonged sojourn in Babylonia.   He bids them build houses and identify themselves with the well-being of the land in which they find themselves.   The period will be seventy years.   It is then that the people may hope for a return. Doubtless Jeremiah intended to suggest at least a couple of generations or so (cf. three* generations in Jer. *27*. 7), though the general use of the number is to indicate a large number as against a small one.   It is, however, the period given in Isa. *23*. 15 as that for which Tyre will be forgotten, 'seventy years, according to the days of one king', the ordinary mortal span of Ps. *90*. 10; as though to say: 'You yourselves will never come back again, but your

---

* The *Epistle of Jeremy* (c. 300 B.C.) has seven generations (*1*. 3).

children.' The same number occurs in Jer. *25*. 12; and 2 Chron. *36*. 21 shows that it was reckoned as the traditional period for the Exile.

But this is not the last that we hear of the seventy years. The figure finds a foremost place in the mind of Zechariah. He refers to the figure in *1*. 12 as the period of the Exile, and again in *7*. 5. It is evident that Zechariah regards the promise made through Jeremiah as due to receive a literal fulfilment in his day, which was roughly seventy years from the first deportation in 597 B.C. This is the attitude in 2 Chron. *36*. 21. In the last chapter of *First Zechariah*, i.e. in *8*. 1–12, we have a glowing picture of the prosperity which will be secured for the returning people of God. Zechariah looks forward to a time of great prosperity under the joint leadership of Jeshua the priest and Zerubbabel the prince (*6*. 9–15), and Haggai also (*2*. 20–23) sees in Zerubbabel the Chosen One of the Lord of Hosts. The terms in which Haggai speaks of the coming triumph are those which we have learned to associate with the coming of the Day of the Lord: 'I will shake the heavens and the earth: and I will overthrow the throne of kingdoms . . .' (*2*. 21f).

Time passes, the Temple is rebuilt, but the glorious Age is as far away as ever. We have no record of anything approaching a national revival until we come to the time of the Maccabees. The 'seventy years' is an unexplained mystery, apart from writers like the writer of 2 Chron. *36*. 21, who is satisfied with the Church-State of post-exilic Jewry with its emphasis on the Temple and its services. But when we come to the *Book of Daniel*, we see an attempt to re-interpret the 'seventy years' of Jeremiah. According to Dan. *9*. 2, they are 'seventy weeks', that is seventy weeks of years. The author has some considerable difficulty in making his figures fit,* but it is clear that

---

* See A. A. BEVAN: *A Short Commentary on the Book of Daniel* (1892), pp. 141–149, in which the general fascination of the figure 'seventy' throughout the centuries is exhibited.

he intends to show that the consummation of the times is
to be found in the victories of Judas Maccabæus.   The end
of the sixty-two weeks of Dan. *9.* 26 is apparently equated
with the murder of Onias II (*c.* 172 B.C.), there having
been a period equivalent to seven weeks before he began
to reckon the sixty-two.   Then the half of the last week
is the 'half a time' in the 'time and times and half a time'
of Dan. *7.* 25.   And here we are led into another calcula-
tion, for the 'time and times and half a time', which at
first seems to have referred to the seven plus sixty-two plus
a last week in two halves, is now taken to mean a year,
two years, and half a year, to make three and a half years,
the forty-two months during which sacrifice ceased in the
time of Antiochus Epiphanes.   This interpretation crops
up in a further re-interpretation in the fifty-two months or
the twelve hundred and sixty days of the *Apocalypse of
John* (*9.* 2, 3; *13.* 5).   When the measurements of the Great
Pyramid are introduced into the calculations the most
surprising results can be achieved!

Another strand of the development is to be found in the
Book of Enoch.   In the section known as *The Apocalypse of
Weeks* (Enoch *93.* 1-14 and *91.* 12-17), a section which is
held to be the oldest portion of the book and pre-Maccabæan, the seventy crops up again, for although the
general mystical scheme is one of ten weeks, yet the fact
that seventy is really involved is clear in *91.* 15 in the
phrase 'in the tenth week in the seventh part', and this is
apart from the fact that ten weeks involves seventy days.
And yet again, as though something had in the result been
found to be wrong with this interpretation, we find the
idea of seventy angels who are successively to preside as
shepherds over the destinies of 'the sheep', to see to it,
amongst other things, that only a limited number of them
fall victim to the malice of their foes (*89.* 59; etc.).

This necessity of re-interpretation is continually recurring.
It is to be found arising out of the identification of the

fourth and last kingdom* in Dan. 7. 7f and 19–25. Here it is identified with the Greek Empire, i.e. that of the Seleucid kings of Antioch. In the *Apocalypse of Baruch* (see 2 Baruch *36.*) there is a vision of a forest, in which after more than one destruction a giant cedar survives. Ultimately the cedar is destroyed, to leave a vine flourishing in the midst of a plain of unfading flowers. We are always safe in identifying the vine with Israel, if only because of Isa. *5.* In the interpretation the giant cedar is equated to the fourth kingdom, and now the fourth kingdom is identified with the Roman empire.

The same re-identification occurs in II (IV) *Esdras* in the explanation of the identity of the winged eagle of the dream of chapter *11.* It is stated in *12.* 11 that 'the eagle, whom thou sawest come up from the sea, is the fourth kingdom which appeared in vision to thy brother Daniel.' The *Apocalypse of Baruch* belongs to the two decades before the Roman War which ended in A.D. 70 with the destruction of the Temple by Titus. The *Ezra Apocalypse* is some twenty years or so later.

All these interpretations look forward to the setting up of an eternal kingdom when the 'seventy years' is fulfilled, whatever the need of each generation may interpret the phrase to mean. The eternity of this kingdom is emphasised in Dan. *2.* 44: 'And in the days of these kings shall the God of heaven set up a kingdom which shall never be destroyed, nor shall the sovereignty thereof be left to another people; . . . and it shall stand for ever.' The same emphasis is to be found in Dan. 7. 14 and 27.

This is the position generally in Jewish apocalypses of the second and first centuries B.C., e.g. Sibylline Oracles *3.* 767 (second century B.C.): 'and then will he raise up a kingdom for all time for all men'; Enoch *62.* 14 (pre-Maccabæan); Jubilees *32* (second century B.C.); Sibylline

---

* See H. H. ROWLEY: *Darius the Mede and the Four World Empires in the Book of Daniel* (1935), pp. 70–137.

Oracles *3*. 46–50 (first century B.C.); and Psalms of Solomon *17*. 4 (middle of first century B.C.).

When, however, we come to the later Jewish apocalypses we find references to a Messianic Kingdom of limited duration, after which the everlasting kingdom will be set up. It is probable that here we are, partly at least, in the realm of Persian influence, for the three thousand years of the Last Age (i.e. the age before the consummation of all things), is divided into periods of a thousand years by the appearance of the Shaoshyants.

It is doubtful whether anything more than the idea of a limited Messianic kingdom on this earth can be ascribed to Iranian influence, though perhaps something of the persistance of the 'thousand' may be due to that origin. The bridge to the idea of a limited kingdom on this earth is to be found in the Apocalypse of Baruch *40*. 3: 'And his principate shall stand for ever, until the world of corruption is at an end, and until the times aforesaid are fulfilled.' The 'thousand' appears also in the extravagant language of *29*. 5: 'The earth also shall yield its fruit ten thousandfold, and on one vine there shall be a thousand branches, and each branch shall produce a thousand clusters, and each cluster shall produce a thousand grapes, and each grape shall produce a *cor* (ninety gallons) of wine.' In the Secrets of Enoch *33* (the Slavonic Enoch, 2 Enoch), written in the first half of the first century A.D., the period of the Messianic Age is a thousand years. This, however, is due to a combination in Jewish interpretation of Gen. *2*. 3 and Ps. *90*. 4; the six days of the Creation followed by the seventh day of rest, combined with, 'For a thousand years in thy sight are but as yesterday when it is past'. The use that is made of this verse from the psalm is illustrated by 2 Pet. *3*. 8: 'One day is with the Lord as a thousand years, and a thousand years as one day.' This period of a thousand years is declared in Rev. *20*. 2–6, e.g. 'But they shall be priests of God and of Christ, and shall reign with him a thousand years'.

But there are other speculations concerning the length of this temporary Messianic kingdom. According to 2 (4) Esdras 7. 28f, the period is four hundred years. The explanation of this figure is given in the Talmud (*Sanhedrin* 99a). It is due to a combination of the four hundred years of affliction in Egypt (Gen. *15*. 13) with Ps. *90*. 15: 'Make us glad according to the days wherein thou hast afflicted us, and the years wherein we have seen evil'. The *Assumption of Moses* (first century A.D.) makes the establishment of the New Age to be one thousand seven hundred and fifty years from the death of Moses, making four and a quarter thousand years from Creation (*1*. 2; *10*, 11). The *Ascension of Isaiah* (end of first century A.D.) has the idea of a temporary Messianic kingdom of three years and seven months and twenty-seven days (*4*. 12), which is the actual 1335 of Dan. *12*. 12, according to the Julian reckoning. Other figures which are found are forty years, three hundred and sixty-five years, six hundred, two thousand, seven thousand years (*b. Sanh.* 97, 99a), all of them based in one way or another on passages of Scripture, perhaps by the combination of two of them.

Thus we see that the figures of the apocalypses are carried on from Age to Age, just as the darkness of the Day of the Lord appears again and again. The same is true of the phraseology generally. This can be seen by a comparison of *Revelation* in the New Testament and *Daniel* in the Old Testament.

CHAPTER XI

MESSIAH

THE development of the figure of Messiah belongs to the post-Old Testament period of Jewish religion, but the origin of the idea is to be found in the earliest times.

The word *Messiah* is actually an adjective formed from the root *mashach*, but in course of time it came to be used first as a title, and at last as a proper name. The root originally means 'wipe, stroke with the hand'. In Hebrew it can be used of smearing a house with paint (Jer. *22*. 14), a shield with oil (2 Sam. *1*. 21. Isa. *21*. 5), and unleavened cakes with oil (Exod. *29*. 2; etc.), but generally it is used of anointing, whether by smearing or by pouring. In Ethiopic the word took another turn, and came to mean 'feast, dine', because of the custom of using oil and sweet-smelling unguents in dressing for feasts (cf. Amos *6*. 6).

The first beginnings of the idea of Messiah belong to the times of primitive religion, when certain persons were supposed to have more-than-human power. The technical name for this power in the text-books on primitive religion is *mana*, a Melanesian word introduced by R. H. Codrington in his study of the folklore and traditions of the inhabitants of the Solomon Islands.* In the Old Testament all such power is ascribed to Jehovah Himself, even though on occasion the results may be surprising to us because of our developed ideas concerning the nature and character of God. The greatest of all the men of antiquity to be imbued with this supernatural power is Moses. 'And there hath not arisen a prophet since in Israel like

* *The Melanesians* (1891).

unto Moses, whom the Lord knew face to face in all the
wonders and the signs which the Lord sent him to do . . .
and in all the mighty hand (i.e. power), and in all the great
terror, which Moses wrought in the sight of all Israel'
(Deut. *34.* 10–12).

There is a close connection between 'anointing' and
'sanctifying' when the latter word (in Hebrew, *hiqdish*) is
used in the sense of separating anything or anyone to the
service of God. The connection is made clear in Num.
7. 1, where, after Moses had set up the tabernacle, he is
described as having 'anointed it and sanctified it'. The
'anointed one' thus becomes the description of a man who
is chosen by God and separated to Him for a particular
purpose. Thus Saul is anointed to be the leader of the
people (1 Sam. *9.* 16), or to be king (1 Sam. *15.* 1). The word
is used generally of kings, the theory being that the king
is called specially by God to rule the people on His behalf.

The custom of anointing priests as a mark of consecration does not appear in the Old Testament until the post-
exilic Priestly Code, and then of the High Priest only.
The holy oil was poured on his head after he had been
robed (Lev. *8.* 12. Ps. *133.* 2), and before the consecration sacrifice.

The first suggestion of this development is to be
found in Zech. *4.* 14, where Zerubbabel the governor,
the scion of the House of David, and Jeshua the High
Priest are called 'the two sons of oil', as the Revised Version
has it correctly, though the Authorised Version has 'the
two anointed ones'.

One factor in this equation of prince and priest, by which
the chief priest comes to be anointed, indeed the dominant
factor, is doubtless to be found in the aim of these early
reformers to set up a theocratic state. This tendency is to
be seen in the last nine chapters of the *Book of the Prophet
Ezekiel*, where the duties of the prince are rigidly prescribed. With the change of policy by Darius I (Hystaspis),

who did away with native princes as rulers, there ceased to be any actual prince of David's line in any sort of position of authority under the Persians. This gave the High Priest more and more authority, so that he did actually become the one representative of God in the government of the people.

There is one instance of the use of the word *mashiach* in connection with the consecration of a prophet in pre-exilic times. This instance is to be found in 1 Kings *19*. 16, where, after Elijah has been bidden to anoint two kings, Jehu over Israel and Hazael over Syria (Damascus), he is told to anoint Elisha, the son of Shaphat of Abel-meholah, to succeed him as prophet. These three men were therefore appointed to execute the Lord's justice upon Ahab and the whole House of Omri. It may be that this was therefore a special rite for a special purpose, and it would be wrong to draw from the incident any conclusion as to the anointing of prophets generally. There is no other evidence of this type except a curious couplet which occurs in Ps. *105*. 15. Here the reference is to the patriarchs, and they are called both 'anointed ones' and 'prophets'. There seems to be no reason why it should be maintained that the psalmist calls them anointed ones (Messiahs) because he is thinking of them as kings. The couplet makes it clear that he is thinking of them as prophets.

The conclusion which we would draw from this is that to be a Messiah means to be called by God to a special function on His behalf. Kings are Messiahs appointed by God to be leaders of the people on behalf of God. The prophets are Messiahs appointed by God to be leaders of the people in matters pertaining more strictly to the Word of God. After the exile, the High Priest is a Messiah to be leader of the people in the days when there was no scion of the House of David who could exercise the Davidic function of ruling God's people.

If it should be held that the prophets are not Messiahs in the general sense which we have indicated, then we must say that Elisha was a Messiah with two others for the special purpose of extirpating the House of Omri that true religion might once more flourish in the land. The patriarchs are Messiahs in Ps. *105*. 15 because in them particularly, as the psalm shows, God made 'known his doings among the peoples'. The Messiah is a divine person in the sense of this special and particular call. We find no evidence of any other sacredness attaching to a Messiah in Israel apart from the fact of this special divine call.

The next stage in the development is to be seen in Isa. *45*. 1, where Cyrus is 'my anointed one' ('my Messiah') in that he is the man whom God has seized with His right hand to humble the Gentiles, loosen the loins of kings so that they bow low in obeisance, and open the prison doors of exile. God has called Cyrus personally ('by name'), and He has given him a title ('surnamed thee'). That title is Messiah, and the special purpose is to set God's people free, this new Jacob-Israel that has been reborn during the Exile. And yet Cyrus never knew the God of Israel, being himself a heathen. Here we get the first suggestion of the identification of a 'Messiah' with a deliverer, for Cyrus's special mission is to deliver Israel from the bondage of exile.

The association of the term Messiah with the idea of a prince of David's line who shall establish God's people at the head of the nations and inaugurate the time of prosperity is to be found in the Psalter. Something indeed is found of it in 2 Sam. *7*, that seed-bed in the Old Testament of all Davidic Messianic ideas. All such passages are ultimately a development of the hopes of Isaiah of Jerusalem, as they are set forth in Isa. *7*. 14f, and especially *9*. 6f, and *11*. 1-9. In the 'messianic' psalms we find this Isaianic strand interwoven with the idea of a 'Messiah' with his special call. In Ps. *2*. 2, for instance, we have the

picture of the heathen kings conspiring against the Lord
and against His anointed. This, presumably, means a
king of David's line. If the psalm is pre-exilic, as is
generally supposed, then the reference is to an actual king
of Judah on whom the psalmist had fixed his hopes of a
glorious reversal of fortune, when Judah should break off
all the bonds of the heathen. Other references are Ps. *18.*
50 (= 2 Sam. *22.* 51); *89.* 36f; *132.* 10 (= 2 Chron. *6.* 42);
132. 18; and also 1 Sam. *2.* 10, 35. These references refer
to the hoped-for deliverer, a king 'anointed of the Lord'
as David was, who shall fulfil all those dreams which
succeeding generations appear to bring no nearer.

The latest reference to a messianic prince in the Old
Testament is Dan. *9.* 25 and 26. Here, however, we are
no farther forward in the development, for the context
makes it plain that the reference in verse 25 is to Jeshua
the High Priest (Zerubbabel's contemporary), and in
verse 26 it is to Onias III, the true High Priest of Maccabæan times, the man who was first deposed by his brother
Joshua (Jason), and later murdered at the instigation of
Menelaus. The use of the word 'prince' to denote the
High Priest in his capacity of ruler of the people is established by Dan. *11.* 22.

Nowhere, therefore, in the Old Testament is the word
'Messiah' used as a title in the sense in which it is found in
the Synoptic Gospels. A passage such as Jer. *30.* 21
undoubtedly had considerable influence in shaping the
content of the idea, but the word 'Messiah' is not found in
it. Or again, there is Ps. *110,* of which the first four verses
are recognised by some as forming an acrostic on the
name Simeon, the brother of Judas Maccabæus, the last
survivor of the five brothers, the man who was acclaimed
'ruler and high priest for ever' in 142 B.C. (1 Macc. *14.* 41).
Here once more we have the expectations of deliverance
and of a future prosperity centred in a particular person,
but no mention of the name 'Messiah'.

Pictures of a time of great prosperity are found elsewhere in connection with the work of a particular person. A notable passage is 1 Macc. *14*. 8–15, descriptive of the golden age introduced by Simon, the Simeon of the acrostic in Ps. *110*. A similar New Age is envisaged under the rule of his son, John Hyrcanus, under whom, after an early eclipse, the sun of Judah shone with an unwonted splendour, e.g. *Testament of the Twelve Patriarchs*, Levi *18*. 2f, and Judah *24*. 1f. John Hyrcanus is the king that 'shall arise in Judah and establish a new priesthood'. Thus the central figure in the deliverance which shall inaugurate the New Age ceases to be a scion of the House of David, and thus of the tribe of Judah, and becomes one of the tribe of Levi, since the Hasmonæans were descended from Levi.

But John Hyrcanus broke with the Pharisees. For the rest of his time, therefore, and during the remainder of the time when the Hasmonæans were ruling, the pious turned away from any idea of a true deliverer and an ideal ruler who should come from the tribe of Levi, of the Hasmonæan stock. Alexander Jannæus, for instance, left little to be desired from the point of view of conquests, or of extending the Jewish authority; but from the point of view of the pious and those who loved the Law he left everything to be desired. And so, during the first century B.C., the hope of a Davidic ruler revived once more. We find this turning once more to the tribe of Judah and the Davidic stock in *Testament XII Patr.*, Judah *24*. 5f, and in the Psalms of Solomon *17*. 23–25, 29f and 36. It is here in *17*. 36 that we get the first use of the name Messiah as the title of the coming king: 'and their king is the Lord Messiah'. The period was a time of disillusionment, when the Pharisees grew more and more to resent the military prowess and ambitions of the Hasmonæan princes. They were emphatic that 'the Lord Messiah' 'will not trust in horsemen or in chariot; nor in the bow: nor shall he multiply to himself gold and silver for war: nor shall he rely on a multitude in the day of war' (verse 37). The same phrase 'the Lord Messiah' occurs also in Psalms of Solomon *18*, which, together with *19*, is not found in the Syriac, but only in the Greek.

We therefore have to think of the term 'the Lord Messiah' as being in use from, say, the first years of the first century B.C., possibly a little earlier. It is the title of the prince through whom the kingdom is to be established. In these Psalms of Solomon there is no suggestion of the heavenly nature of Messiah. He is to be a prince who shall arise in the ordinary course of events. At any rate, the title is not found here in any apocalyptic setting.

THE SON OF MAN.

There is another strand of expectation concerning the advent of the kingdom, and with it another conception of the leading figure in its establishment. This is the apocalyptic setting with its conception of the Son of Man. The beginning of this idea is to be found in the well-known vision in Dan. 7. There the seer saw 'in the night visions, and behold there came with the clouds of heaven one like unto a son of man . . . and there was given him dominion and glory, and a kingdom, that all the peoples, nations, and languages should serve him: his dominion is an everlasting dominion, which shall not pass away, and his kingdom that which shall not be destroyed' (verses 13, 14). In Dan. 7. 27 this figure 'like unto a son of man' is interpreted to mean 'the people of the saints of the Most High'. The phrase 'a son of man' has thus what is called a 'messianic' significance, the word 'messianic' being used to describe general ideas of an age of great prosperity for the Jews. But it has no reference to a personal Messiah; indeed it has no personal reference at all.

The personal significance of 'the Son of Man' is to be found in the *Book of Enoch*. The identification of 'that

Son of Man' and 'the anointed' of the Lord of Spirits is to be found in Enoch *48.* 1–10, especially in verses 2 and 10. This passage is generally agreed to belong to the period from 105–64 B.C., i.e. roughly the period of Psalms of Solomon *17,* possibly a little later.   Other names are used in this same section, namely the Righteous One (*38.* 2) and the Elect One (*40.* 5).   These are to be found in Acts *3.* 14 and in Luke *9.* 35.   The germane passages in the *Book of Enoch* are *46.* 1, 3, 4; *45.* 3; *48.* 2–10; *49.* 2; *69.* 27ff, all of them belonging to the same section, first half of the first century B.C.   The Son of Man is a supernatural figure. His 'name was named before the Lord of Spirits', 'before the sun and the signs were created, before the stars of the heaven were made' (*48.* 2).   He sits on the throne of God (*51.* 3), which becomes his own throne also (*62.* 2 and 3, 5, with *69.* 27, 29).   All judgement is committed to this Son of Man (*41.* 9; *69,* 27), and he is to rule over all, so 'that the kings and the mighty and all who possess the earth shall bless and glorify and extol him' (*62.* 6).

There are those who deny that the phrase 'Son of Man' has any personal significance in the *Book of Enoch,* and that there, as in the *Book of Daniel,* it stands for 'the people of the saints of the Most High', i.e. the true Israel.*   Others deny that it was ever intended as a title at all, but that it stands for an Aramaic idiom to signify 'a frail child of man, whom God would make Lord of the world' (*Dalman*).

The larger number of scholars would agree that in *Daniel* the Son of Man is not an individual figure, but that quite naturally there should be such a figure, regarded as the leader of the triumphant saints in the new kingdom. This personal aspect comes clearly to the front in the *Book of Enoch.*   All this is in an apocalyptic setting, and the leader of the kingdom is one who comes 'from above'.

* See especially T. W. MANSON: *The Teaching of Jesus* (1931), pp. 211–236.   Earlier discussion is summarised by S. R. Driver, art. 'Son of Man' in *Hastings' Bible Dictionary,* s.c., pp. 579–589; also H. H. ROWLEY: *The Relevance of Apocalyptic* (1944), pp. 29f, etc.

There is no clear evidence that the Son of Man was
equated with Messiah before the time of Jesus, though we
are inclined to think with Albright that there was some
fusion.* We would say that the tendency was to think
of Messiah as the Prince of the kingdom in so far as it was
thought of as coming to pass more or less in the course of
this world's history, whilst there was the corresponding
tendency to think of the Son of Man as the Leader of the
kingdom in so far as it was all thought of as coming from
above by the direct intervention of God. It seems to us
that it is difficult to say in respect of a great deal of the
apocalyptic language just to what extent it was intended
as exact description, and just to what extent it was taken
as symbolical. On these grounds it seems probable that
there was a connection between the two terms even before
the time of Jesus. It is sometimes said that Jesus combined
the idea of the Son of Man with that of the Suffering Servant
but there is an association established in Enoch *48*. 4
where, in reference to the Son of Man, it is said of him that
'he shall be a light of the Gentiles' (cf. Isa. *42*. 6; *49*. 6.
Luke *2*. 32). In any case, it is clear that there has been
some considerable development in the content of the ideas
of both Messiah and Son of Man during the fifty years each
side the beginning of our era. The seeds of that development are to be found in the approaches to identification
in the *Book of Enoch*.

* *From the Stone Age to Christianity* (1940), p. 292.

CHAPTER XII

LIFE AFTER DEATH

IS there any survival after death? This is a question which moderns ask. Primitive peoples never asked such a question. They assumed that there was some sort of survival of the human spirit after death, though shadowy and probably not for long. Almost all peoples have believed in the survival of the individual for at least a limited time. We find it advisable to draw a distinction between 'immortality' and 'survival', because the former word infers that the human spirit was regarded as never dying at all.

There is a certain amount of evidence to suggest that, amongst primitive peoples, those individuals who possessed *mana*,* survived in greater degree according to the extent to which they were men of *mana*. But even these heroes were not generally assumed to live on indefinitely in the spirit world. It may indeed be the case that the hero who is worshipped lived in the very remote past, but where investigation is possible, it has often been found that the hero-ancestor belonged to the not-very-remote past. The cult of the hero-ancestor lasts as long as the memory of their *mana* remains. Apart from the most exceptional instances, they are gradually relegated more and more into the shadowy, uncertain limbo of the dead.

Further, it is not the case that all peoples everywhere have believed in the survival of the individual. The outstanding case is that of the Arunta, an Australian tribe

* A Melanesian word introduced by R. H. CODRINGTON: *The Melanesians* (1891) to denote that more-than-human power with which special people were credited. See p. 106.

now largely extinct, but famous in the study of primitive religion as being the one 'unspoilt' Stone Age people of whom we have anything like full details. The Arunta have had a strange belief whereby they regard their newborn children as being reincarnations of Alcheringa ancestors, that is, strange beings who were supposed to roam the Australian wastes in the Golden Age which these aborigines believed to have existed before the first man proper was born. These curious beliefs have precluded a 'straight' belief in individuality, and with this strange disbelief there have developed curious ideas of reincarnation.

But amongst the Hebrews there was always a belief in some sort of existence after death, though this was far from being anything in the nature of immortality. Indeed, nowhere, either in the Old Testament or in the New Testament, is there any doctrine of immortality in the true sense of the term. For when the Hebrews came to have definite ideas of life after death these were ideas of resurrection rather than of immortality.

The earliest beliefs of the Hebrews are embodied in the phrase 'being gathered to their fathers'. This is the phrase that is found in Judges 2. 10. The statement is made of Joshua's generation, and it is found in a paragraph which is recognised as belonging to the E tradition. The later phrase is 'being gathered to his (their) people'. This is the phrase that is found in the P tradition, e.g. Gen. 25. 8, 17; 35. 29; 49. 29, 33. Num. 20. 24, 26, etc. Deut. 32. 50. To what extent this actually meant any real life beyond the grave cannot be definitely estimated. It is commonly assumed that it involves some sort of conscious fellowship, however tenuous. But this is somewhat discounted by 2 Kings 22. 20, with its equivalent 2 Chron. 34. 28; where we read: 'I will gather thee to thy fathers, and thou shalt be gathered to thy grave in peace.' Whether the former phrase is to be regarded as determinative for the second phrase or vice versa is probably a matter for discussion, but the verse at any rate suggests that there was a mode of thought, persisting into post-exilic times, which regarded death as the end of all activity, a time of rest, perhaps of oblivion, in the grave in company with those who had gone that way before. This is all the more likely because we know that the Sadducees of the time of Our Lord did not accept any doctrine of the resurrection of the dead.

There was, however, in earlier days a persistent practice of consulting the dead, a custom which at first seems to have been allowed to be legitimate, but which every orthodox king is said to have done his best to eliminate. Saul had done his best to uproot necromancy in Israel, but in his desperation he sought out the witch of Endor, I Sam. 28. 3-25. The woman is bidden to call up Samuel. Here is a case of one being 'raised' who was not long dead, and who was known to have been a man mighty in *mana*. Whether any dead man could be so called up is open to question, but Samuel certainly is thought of as still retaining sufficient 'life-stuff' to appear to the woman, though not apparently to Saul (verse 13f). Here we get clear evidence of a cult of the dead amongst the Israelites, though it is far from being ancestor-worship in the sense in which anthropologists use the term. We have, of course, to allow for the revising activity of succeeding generations, who may naturally be supposed to have omitted much in earlier practice which did not accord with later ideas, but the evidence which survives suggests in itself nothing more than a limited survival, and only on the part of one who was exceptionally endowed with *mana*. The warning against necromancy in the fragment Isa. 8. 19 is indecisive on this particular point.

Apart from this case of Samuel, we find references elsewhere to the *repha'im*.* The word is comparatively late

* The same word is used of an old race of giants, formerly inhabitants of Canaan, Gen. 15. 20; Josh. 17. 15 (both JE), and later.

in the Old Testament, e.g. Job *26*. 5, as the name of the
dead, and also in Isa. *14*. 9; *26*. 14, 19. Ps. *88*. 10.
Prov. *2*. 18; *9*. 18; *21*. 16.   The word is generally supposed
to be derived from the root *raphah* (sink down, relax).*
These 'shades' are regarded as being in Sheol (Isa. *14*. 9.
Prov. *9*. 18) or in the earth (Isa. *26*. 18).   They are regarded in the comparatively late Isa. *26*. 18 as having some
sort of permanence, else even the dead of righteous Israel
could not be cast forth from the earth.

The general ideas concerning the dead in earlier times
fall, then, into two groups, both of which may well have
been accepted at the same time.   On the one hand, we
have the idea of a man being gathered to his fathers,
buried in the grave with them, and all of them being at
rest together.   Coupled with this is the idea that the dead
tend to retain some life during the period immediately
following death.   This idea receives support from recent
archæological work in Palestine, where it is customary to
find every kind of utensil buried with the dead for their
use after death.   The dead needed food and drink; they
needed life-giving blood, and a case is known where human
sacrifice was made on behalf of the dead in order that the
dead might partake of the life of the living.   This was at
Gezer.†   On the other hand, and running parallel with
all these ideas, which are connected directly with the grave,
we have a developing idea of Sheol as the underground and
roomy home of the dead.   The idea seems to have
developed roughly in the time of the early prophets, from
(say) the ninth century B.C. onwards, and it persisted right
through Biblical times.

The idea of Sheol may well have associations with Babylonian ideas, where the abode of the dead is described in

* Oesterley would connect it with the root *rapha'* and take it to
mean 'healers', *The Jews and Judaism during the Greek Period* (1941),
p. 178.   We find this suggestion to be unconvincing and without
adequate support.
† Palestine Exploration Fund Report, 1902.

terms which are strongly reminiscent of the kind of thing we find in parts of the Old Testament. Sheol was regarded as being as far below the earth as the heavens are high above it, the two being extremes, Ps. *139*. 8. Isa. *7*. 11. Amos *9*. 2. It is a land of darkness and deep shadow, from which there is no return (Job. *10*. 21. Prov. *2*. 19). It is a place of darkness, without hope, where the worm is mother and sister of the dead (Job. *17*. 13f.), a place of dust and worms (Job *21*. 26). A gruesome picture of the hopelessness and the lifelessness of Sheol is drawn in Isa. *14*. 9. This is the taunt-song against Babylon, once so mighty that the whole earth was unquiet. At last Babylon has ceased to be, and her king is dead. 'Sheol from beneath is moved for thee to meet thee at thy coming; it stirreth up the shades (*repha'im*) for thee, even all the chief ones of earth; it hath raised up from their thrones all the kings of the nations. All they shall answer and say to thee, Art thou become weak as we? art thou become like unto us?' Here, it is true, the shades of the mighty have some sort of life, but it is a pale shadow of life on earth. They do certainly act there as they acted here, but all in a listlessness that is weakness beyond words.

Against this background there developed an idea of a real life after death, but such an idea of a resurrection life was by no means universal. We have said that the Sadducees of New Testament times did not accept any such doctrine (Matt. *22*. 23; etc.). They held by the ancient traditional Sheol doctrine.

Strictly speaking the passages in the Old Testament which clearly speak of a resurrection life after death are no more than two in number.* They are Isa. *26*. 19 and Dan. *12*. 2. The first passage (Isa. *26*. 19) is: 'Thy dead shall live; my (probably 'the') corpses shall arise; they

---

* This is the opinion of H. Wheeler Robinson. See his post-humously published *Inspiration and Revelation in the Old Testament* (1946), p. 101.

shall awake and they shall shout for joy, they that dwell
in the dust; for the dew of herbs (?) is their dew, and the
earth shall give birth to (lit. 'cause to fall') shades
(*repha'im*)'. Here we get an assurance that the dead
martyrs of Israel shall arise to partake in the blessings of the
Great Day. The prophet doubtless includes all true
Israelites, those who have died in tribulation and in
persecution during the dark days. The date of the passage
is variously estimated, and some would put it as late as the
close of the second century B.C. It is certainly not earlier
than the beginning of the third century. This idea of the
resurrection of the martyrs of Israel is developed in
Enoch *61*. 5, where all the elect will 'return and stay themselves on the day of the Elect One', 'those who have been
destroyed by the desert, and those who have been devoured
by beasts, and those who have been devoured by the fish
of the sea.'

The second passage, Dan. *12*. 2, sets forth unmistakably
a resurrection from the dead, both of the wicked and of
the righteous. It belongs to the second century B.C., and
reads 'and many of them that sleep in the dust of the earth
shall awake, some to everlasting life and some to shame and
everlasting contempt'.

There are other passages also which some scholars judge
to refer to a life after death. One of these is Ps. *139*. 7-12.
'Whither shall I go from thy spirit? or whither shall I
flee from thy presence? If I ascend to the heavens, there
art thou; if I make my couch in Sheol, behold thou art
there. If I take the wings of the dawn, and dwell in the
uttermost parts of the sea, even there shall thy hand lead
me, and thy right hand shall hold me.' We do not find
here any suggestion of life after death, but rather a growing
belief in God's omnipresence. There is no place, high in
the heavens above, deep down in the earth beneath, far
away as the ocean is wide, no place at all where God's
guiding hand is not to be found. The idea that God has

power in Sheol would certainly be a step on towards a belief in the resurrection of the dead, but we would hold that the reference here is geographical, and not at all theological.

Another passage which some have held to be a statement of a belief in a life after death is Ps. *73*. 24f: 'Thou shalt guide me with thy counsel, and afterward receive me to (R.V. 'with') glory. Whom have I in the heavens but thee? and there is none on earth that I desire beside thee.' A reference to life after death is more apparent in the English Versions than it is in the Hebrew, or even in the rendering just given, where we have replaced 'heaven' by the more correct rendering 'the heavens'. Once again the reference is geographical. The phrase 'afterward receive me to glory' most naturally means 'bring me to honour (*kabod*) and prosperity after my present troubles are over.' We do not see any possibility of the word *kabod* (glory) being intended by the psalmist to mean heavenly bliss, nor do we find any reference in the psalm to life after death. The psalmist's confidence is that though his own feet had well nigh slipped, and he had almost given up hope, yet when he went into the Sanctuary of God, then there was vouchsafed to him a vision of the end. The wicked would come to sudden death, whereas he himself, because of his righteousness, would afterwards (i.e. after his troubles were over) be received to prosperity. No longer would it be the wicked who 'have more than heart could wish' (verse 7).

Yet another passage around which considerable controversy in this connection has raged is Job *19*. 25f. Unfortunately the Hebrew text in this passage is far from easy, and there is every indication that there is some corruption. Verse 25 is tolerably secure, where Job says: 'I know that my redeemer (i.e. vindicator) liveth, and that he will stand up at the last upon the dust.' That is, Job is very sure that there is one who will show that he is in the right and will establish his cause on this earth. Many take 'the dust' to refer to the dust of Job's grave, but we do not find this to be a Hebrew point of view at all. 'Dust' is quite a legitimate contrast to 'heaven' (cf. Job 4. 18f), and this, we take it, is what the writer meant. It is the first line of verse 26 which is so difficult; indeed, strictly speaking it is untranslatable, and almost all scholars find themselves resorting to emendation in an attempt to make it into reasonably correct Hebrew. It is just possible to translate, 'and after my skin has thus been struck off, then from my flesh I shall see God'. No Hebrew scholar, however, feels quite comfortable about this; it is just barely possible to get this rendering out of the Hebrew. We take the line to mean that though the whole of Job's skin be shredded off him in his foul disease, yet even then he is sure that from his flesh (i.e. from his bare flesh, stripped of his covering of skin, or, though his disease reach its worst possible stage) he will come face to face with God.

The only way to see in the Hebrew any reference to life after death is to translate 'away from my flesh' and then it must be supposed that it is Job's disembodied spirit that will see God. Such an idea scarcely belongs to the Old Testament idea of what life after death could be. The Hebrew could not conceive of any sort of spirit existing without some sort of a body, as witness Paul's argument in 1 Cor. 15. 35ff, where he has first to demonstrate that there can be different kinds of bodies, and only then can he go on to argue for a resurrection. To think of a spirit apart from a body involves importing into the context ideas which are alien to the whole Jewish conception of the psychology of man. To the Hebrews, man is a body animated by a life-soul (*nephesh*), and when the man is dead, there is no life-soul anywhere. All that remains is the listless shadow in Sheol, without life, without desire, without everything except the shadow. And even when a resurrection life is mentioned in the Old Testament, it comes through the revivifying of that very body of flesh which, on this translation, Job has left behind. The idea of a disembodied Job apart from his flesh could never have arisen before Greek ideas of an indestructible human soul had infiltrated into Jewish thinking. This was long after the time when the *Book of Job* was written, and it is doubtful whether such an idea ever took root amongst orthodox Jews. (See below p. 127).

The conclusion of the matter is that the idea of life after death is a late development of Hebrew thought, belonging to the very latest stratum of the Old Testament. The idea is not earlier than the third century B.C. at the earliest, and most scholars would not allow it to be earlier than the second century. Even then we get such a writer as the author of *Ecclesiastes* envisaging one doom for all things living, whether man or beast. 'Of the wise man, even as of the fool, there is no remembrance for ever' (*2*. 16), 'for that which befalleth the sons of men befalleth beasts; even one thing befalleth them: as one dieth, so dieth the other; yea, they have all one breath (*ruach*, 'spirit that gives life'); and man hath no pre-eminence above the beasts' (*3*. 19).

The doctrine of a resurrection life arises out of the gradual acceptance of the idea of a Day of Judgement at the end of the world era. Both the passages mentioned above, Isa. *26*. 19 and Dan. *12*. 2, are in that kind of context. We get an early form of the idea in the picture of the Grand Assize in the valley of Jehoshaphat where God will sit to judge all the nations(Joel *3*. 12). So long as there is no particular emphasis on retribution, then there is no thought of any real life beyond death apart from that of a shadowy Sheol. When the idea of retribution first arises it is envisaged as taking place in this life. This we understand to be the teaching of Ps. *73*. 24 and also in Job *19*. 25f. The idea of individual retribution arises from Ezek. *18*. 19–32. When sad experience had taught the individual

Israelite that in this life there can be no guarantee of either rewards for the righteous or punishment for the wicked, then he began to look for another world in which these matters of justice would receive proper attention. Similarly, when generation after generation passed by, and Israel still found herself to be the tail and not the head,* then again Israel began to look for another world in which this matter of justice also would receive proper attention. And so we find the hope expressed that the dead Israelites who had shared only Israel's reproach would be raised up from their sleeping-place in the earth in order to share Israel's glory also. This is expressed in the Maccabæan Enoch *90*. 32–36, under the figure of sheep, scattered and destroyed, but all at last gathered, their wool white and abundant and clean.

Here we find the effect of the Persian ideas of the Coming Age. It meant in Israel, as in Persia, first of all a fire and then a general judgement. But whereas amongst the Persians there may have been a belief that in the end all would be saved at last through the refining fire, amongst the Jews the resurrection of the wicked was a resurrection to condemnation and punishment without relief.

The idea of an extension of the field for retribution beyond this life is to be found in Enoch *22*. 9–13, a portion which belongs to the earlier part of the second century B.C. It is therefore roughly contemporary with the *Daniel* passage (*12*. 2), where there is envisaged a resurrection to life for the righteous and to everlasting contempt for the wicked. The Enoch passage refers to the hollow places, which Enoch's angel guide tells him 'have been made so that the spirits of the dead might be separated'. There is one division for the spirits of the righteous 'in which there is the bright spring of water'. A second division in Sheol is for the spirits of those who have not suffered retribution on earth for their sins. These will be in great pain until

* See *The Book of Enoch 103*. 9–15.

the day of judgement, when they will be delivered over to a punishment yet more severe. The third division is for those who have suffered a full retribution in life. These shall not be raised in the Day of Judgement, nor will they be slain. They remain in Sheol for ever. In the Apocalypse of Moses *37*. 5; *40*. 1, (first century A.D.) the Paradise where the righteous await the Last Day is in the Third Heaven (cf. 2 Cor. *12*. 2).

We thus see how the belief in a resurrection from Sheol is connected with the idea of individual retribution. The Enoch passage which we have just mentioned (*22*. 9-13) looks for a resurrection only for those for whom some adjustment needs to be made after death. For those who have received on earth the full penalty for their sins there is no resurrection. But for those who have not received the true and proper retribution, whether for good or for ill, there is a resurrection in order that all may be 'equal', as Ezek. *18* puts it. The assumption by this time is that all the righteous receive stripes in this world. And this same desire for a just and proper retribution has led to the idea of divisions in Sheol, and especially of a place of punishment there.

The idea of exact and precise retribution dominates the *Book of Jubilees* (time of the Maccabee rising). For instance, in *4*. 31, Cain receives an exact retribution, 'for with a stone he killed Abel, and with a stone he was killed in righteous judgement'. It is worked out in connection with the final judgement in *5*. 15: 'In regard to all He will judge, the great according to his greatness, the small according to his smallness, and each according to his way'.

The idea of a resurrection, some to glory and some to shame, is found also in the *Testaments of the Twelve Patriarchs*, Benjamin *10*. 6-9, a section which undoubtedly has received additions by Christian editors. First the Old Testament patriarchs will rise, and 'then', so the original reads, 'shall we also rise', and 'all be changed, some unto glory and some unto shame. And the Lord shall judge Israel first, for their unrighteousness, and then so shall he judge all the Gentiles'. The Christian interpolation is that He will judge Israel, 'for when He appeared as God in the flesh to deliver them, they believed Him not', and the further statement that He will judge the Gentiles, 'as many as believed Him not when He appeared upon earth'.

There are innumerable passages to be found in the writings of the first century B.C. which deal with the idea of a resurrection in connection with the day of judgement, and with the concern for individual retribution. In the first century A.D. the references are multiplied. Especially they are to be found in the *Ezra Apocalypse*, i.e. in II (IV) Esdras *3–14* of the *Apocrypha*. In 7. 32–36, for instance, we find again a reference to the 'secret places' (the hollow places) of Enoch *22*. 3, combined with other ideas of an earlier date: 'and the earth shall restore those that are asleep in her; and so shall the dust those that dwell therein in silence'. Or again, in the same passage we find reference to a resurrection of both good and bad in the Day of Judgement. The earlier tendency was to believe that only the righteous rise in order that they might partake of the blessedness of the New Age. This is the general view in *Enoch* and it is found also in the Psalms of Solomon *3*. 13–16. Such a persistence of an older idea shows the way in which the various writers were feeling forward to something more definite, or to some fuller doctrine concerning these matters. The idea survives even in the first century A.D. *Apocalypse of Moses* (*28*. 4), where God says to Adam: 'yet when thou art gone out of Paradise, if thou shouldst keep thyself from all evil, as one about to die, when again the resurrection hath come to pass I will raise thee up and then there shall be given to thee the tree of life'. But according to the slightly earlier (first half of first century A.D.) *Secrets of Enoch*, there is a place prepared for every soul (*49*. 2) and innumerable mansions 'good for the good and bad for the bad' (*61*. 2).

When we come to this first century A.D. we also find the idea growing of a clear distinction between the body and the spirit. Before this the prevalent idea is that of a bodily resurrection, and the spirit is that which animates the flesh. At death this spirit will 'return unto God who gave it' (Eccles. *12*. 7). There are some twenty-five cases altogether where the word *ruach* (spirit) is used for the breath-soul (usually *nephesh*).* The earliest such passages are to be found in the *Book of Job* and in the Priestly Code (though here only in the form 'God of the spirits of all flesh', Num. *16*. 22 ; *27*. 16), apart from the isolated Ps. *31*. 5 : 'Into thine hand I commit my spirit'. In *Ecclesiastes* the idea of both man and beast having a 'spirit' is frequently expressed, though here the word is used as equivalent to *nephesh* (breath-soul, the Latin *anima*). The usage grows as the years pass by, and is due mostly to the influence of the idea, inherent and necessary where the idea of retribution is involved, of some sort of continuity between the living body on earth and the resurrected body after death, though Greek ideas that there is in man an imperishable element (the 'soul') may have had something to do with it. In the *Book of Enoch* we find references to the 'spirits' of men, both of the good and of the bad. In the first century B.C. sections of *Enoch* (The Similitudes, *37–71*), we have the picture of the righteous being clothed with 'garments of glory', or 'garments of life from the Lord of spirits' (*62*. 16). Or again, in the *Ascension of Isaiah* (first century A.D.), we find it stated clearly that they will be 'stripped of the garments of flesh' and robed 'in their garments of the upper world' 'like angels standing there in great glory'. Similarly in the first century A.D. *Ezra Apocalypse* (*7*. 88), the body is referred to as 'the corruptible vessel'. All this kind of thing brings us directly into

* See my *The Distinctive Ideas of the Old Testament* (1944), p. 148.

the world of St. Paul and that of the New Testament generally.

A still further development is to be found in the Secrets of Enoch *23*. 5 (A.D. 1–50): 'All souls are prepared to eternity' before the foundation of the world. Here we can see the influence of the Platonic doctrine of the immortality of the soul, pre-natal as well as post-mortal. It came into Jewish thought via Egypt, and is expressed clearly in Wisdom of Solomon *8*. 19f (between 217 and 145 B.C. in Egypt): 'Now I was a goodly child, and a goodly soul fell to my lot: Nay rather, being good, I came into a body undefiled.' Philo co-opted this doctrine as well as many other Greek ideas until the idea emerges, in later Jewish books, that these unborn souls dwelt in the seventh heaven (so the Talmud, *Chagigah* 12b) or in a special chamber (so the Midrash *Sifre* 143b) until they were called to enter human bodies.

On the contrary, we have the opposite view prevailing, whereby it is emphasised that the body is of the greatest importance so far as the life after death is concerned. In the first century A.D. *Life of Adam and Eve* (*48*. 1), and in the *Apocalypse of Moses* (*37*. 4–*40*. 7), two books which are strangely intertwined, we find Michael the archangel put in special charge of the body of Adam, to which is added also the body of righteous Abel, and he has, according to some authorities, three other archangels to assist him. And even in the Syriac *Apocalypse of Baruch* (last half of the first century A.D.) *49*. 2–*51*. 6, we have a belief in the actual resurrection of the body, where the dead are raised up without any change in their bodies, the earth giving them up just as it received them. In this way those yet alive will see for themselves that the dead have been raised, and will be able to recognise them (cf. Matt. *27*. 52f). Then those who have 'been justified will have their aspect changed into splendour and beauty' (cf. 1 Cor. *15*. 35–50), and 'the aspect of those who now act wickedly shall become worse than it is, as they shall suffer torment'.

There remains now to give some idea of the development of the way in which the fate of the wicked and of the righteous came to be pictured. We have seen, in Enoch 22. 9-13, the beginning of the idea of Hell as a place of punishment and torment. This is in the idea of the three hollow places in Sheol, one of which is for the righteous, another for the wholly neutral, and the third a place of torment and retribution for unrighteous men who have continued to prosper on earth, and in whose death, as Ps. 73. 4 puts it, there were no pangs. In this picture there is no thought of any 'second chance' beyond the grave. The hollow place to which the spirit of the dead man is committed at death is irrevocably fixed at the time of his death, determined by the actions of his life on earth. Everything depends upon his record. If he has been righteous, then his spirit is held in some sort of pleasant suspended animation till the Day of Judgement. If he has been unrighteous, then his fate depends upon whether or not he has suffered retribution on earth for his sins.

Parallel with the idea of Sheol is the idea of Gehenna, as the Greek New Testament spells it. The origin of the name and the idea is to be found in Ge Hinnom ('the valley of Hinnom'), a valley to the west of Jerusalem, which at one time was the scene of child sacrifice (Jer. 7. 31f). In those days it was called (probably) Tapheth, the spelling Topheth being due to the custom of the scribes to insert the vowels of the word *bosheth* (shame) into any name that had idolatrous associations. It came to be the general rubbish heap, always on fire, the place where 'the worm dieth not and the fire is not quenched'. At one time the phrase 'to be cast into Gehenna' may well have meant nothing more than to be cast out as useless, but it naturally became combined with the Persian ideas of the refining fire at the Last Day, the fire which, according

to the Persians was to purge away all dross. It remained, however, for the Jews, a fire of retribution, and
even of punishment without the thought of cleansing.
The tendency was to combine the idea of Gehenna with
that place in Sheol where the wicked were in great pain,
those wicked who had not received on earth the just
retribution for their sins. The deep valley of Ge Hinnom
with its burning fire is thus transferred to Sheol (Enoch 54.
1–3; 90. 26f.), though even more accurately it is that place
of endless torment whither these wicked are cast after the
judgement. The identification is by no means thorough
and complete, and Gehenna is sometimes used as the
equivalent of at least part of Sheol and sometimes as that
other dreadful place of endless punishment.

On the other hand a growingly glorious picture is painted
of the abode of the righteous. They will dwell 'in the
garden of life' (Enoch 61. 12), that is, in that Garden from
which man was excluded in the first days when sin and
death entered into the world. In the Apocalypse of
Abraham 21 (end of first century A.D.), we find the full
equation of the abode of the righteous and the Garden of
Eden: 'And I saw there the Garden of Eden and its fruits,
the source of the stream issuing from it, and its trees and
their bloom, and those who have behaved righteously, and
I saw therein their foods and blessedness. And I saw
there a great multitude . . .' Here, then, we get the idea
of Paradise* as the abode of the righteous. It is here not
an intermediate state, but the abode of the righteous for
ever. Further, there seems to be no indication that this
abode of the blessed is to be anywhere other than on earth.
It is to be a renewed earth, as in Enoch 45. 5, where the
earth will be transformed and made a blessing, 'and I will
cause mine elect to dwell in it'.

* A Persian word, used of the great landscape gardens in which
the Persian kings delighted, containing every kind of tree. The
word finds its way into this context through the Septuagint translation of Gen. 2. 3.

All this is seen to be the general background of the New Testament ideas. We find the rich man suffering in Hades-Sheol (Luke *16*. 19–31) because he had died with his ill-gotten wealth, and had not suffered retribution before death. On the other hand, Lazarus, the righteous man who had not seen 'good' on earth, is 'in Abraham's bosom', awaiting the Day of Judgement, but with a great gulf fixed between him and Dives, so that neither can come near the other. Or again, we have the reference in John *14*. 2 to the places that are prepared for the righteous. Perhaps the promise to come again and receive them to Himself is a promise to take them at the Last Day from the abiding-places for the righteous to the abode of the blessed.

The general tendency of the New Testament is to speak of the resurrection of the righteous, for both body and soul can be destroyed in Gehenna (Matt. *10*. 28). In Mark *9*. 43–49 the single-eyed enter into life, while those who stumble are cast into Gehenna. According to Luke *20*. 35, only those who are accounted worthy can attain to the resurrection of the dead and the life of the world to come. And the resurrection is of those who are 'in Christ' or 'those that are Christ's at His coming', 1 Cor. *15*. 22f. On the other hand, in John *5*. 28f, we have a double resurrection, 'a resurrection of life'. and 'a resurrection of judgement'.

CHAPTER XIII

DEMONS AND ANGELS

POST-EXILIC Judaism saw the beginning of a strong
development towards dualism. This is evidenced first
in the development of the character of Satan, and afterwards in the development of whole ranks upon ranks of
demons and angels, all in descending order of importance.

The character who later comes to be the Devil appears
first in the prologue of the *Book of Job*. Here he is 'the
Satan', one of 'the sons of God'. This latter phrase is a
literal translation of the ordinary Hebrew idiom for denoting
a class of beings. The Satan is one of a group of supernatural beings who are regarded as forming God's heavenly
court, His servants to do His bidding. The word *satan*
means 'adversary', and his task is to walk to and fro in the
earth, testing men to see if they are really as good as they
pretend to be. His further task is to accuse them before
the judgement seat of God.

But already we find that the Satan has ceased to show
much semblance of true neutrality. His experience has
caused him to hold that there is no man who is truly and
disinterestedly righteous. Even Job, 'perfect and upright' as God claims him to be, is good only because it
pays. The Satan is quite sure that there is no such thing
amongst men as true piety. He is thus the accuser
(*diabolos*) of the whole race of men. But God is so sure
that Job is disinterestedly pious that he permits the Satan
to test Job. Thus develops the picture of the Satan as not
only the accuser (*diabolos*) of men, but also the tester
(*peirazōn*), a word which easily slips over into the meaning

'tempt', all the more easily because in the *Septuagint* it is the equivalent of the Hebrew *nissah*, a word which has both meanings. And so the Satan inflicts upon Job one disaster after another, until Job is stripped of all his possessions and all his children. Finally Job is overtaken by every calamity short of death itself, so much so that death becomes to him the greatest of blessings. In the end Job is vindicated, but we hear no more of the Satan after the prologue. Perhaps this is because already the Satan's function has become wholly condemnatory.

The figure of the Satan appears again in an early post-exilic writing, namely in Zech. *3.* 1–9. This passage is probably earlier than the larger part of the *Book of Job*, but it may not be earlier than the prologue. In any case, earlier or not in the historical sense, the idea is more developed than in the prologue to *Job*. Here also in Zech. *3*, the word Satan is not a proper name, but remains descriptive of the office. He is still 'the Satan'. He stands as accuser of Jeshua the High Priest, who stands before the angel of God arrayed in filthy garments as though degraded from the priesthood. Judgement is given by the angel of God in favour of Jeshua, and he is established in his high-priesthood. The Satan is still man's accuser before God, but here he is rebuked because he is a false accuser. This becomes more and more his reputation. The same development takes place in the significance of the Hebrew word *satan* as that which had taken place in the case of the Greek word *diabolos*. This word very soon, even in secular Greek, came to have a bad meaning, and to be used in the sense of 'false accuser, traducer'. It is used in this sense of Haman the enemy of the Jews in the Septuagint version of Esther *7.* 1, though in the Septuagint of Ps. *108* (Hebrew *109*). 6 it is used in a 'good' sense, that is, in the sense of an accuser who is speaking the truth though it be bad. The Hebrew here has *satan*.

The final development of the idea of the Satan in the Old

Testament is to be found in 1 Chron. *21.* 1.   Here Satan
(for the word has by this time become a proper name) is
the adversary of God and not of man only.   He it is who
tempted David to number the people, and so enticed him
into conduct deemed contrary to the will of God.   The
passage should be compared with 2 Sam. *24.* 1, where it is
said that God Himself enticed David, and then punished
him.   Later it was evidently realised that such conduct
was scarcely seemly for God, and so the unenviable deed
was credited to Satan, by this time the enemy of God
Himself, always ready to tempt man into disobedience and
sin.

In the books outside the Old Testament we find a further
development of the character of Satan.   In the *Book of
Enoch* (in the Similitudes, first half of the first century B.C.),
he is the king of the counter-kingdom of evil and is wholly
at enmity with God.   In the earlier parts of the book we
read of the Satans who led astray the fallen angels and all
mankind (*69.* 4, 6).   In the Similitudes (Enoch *37–71*)
these are identified with the angels of punishment, who
abide in a deep yawning valley, where they are 'preparing
all the instruments of Satan' (*53.* 4), with which the kings
and the mighty ones of earth are to be destroyed.   These
'instruments of Satan', 'iron chains of immeasurable
weight', are made in a 'deep valley with burning fire'
(*54.* 2, 3), the Gehenna of apocalyptic lore.   The Satans
can appear before God and accuse men, just as did the
Satan of the prologue of Job and of Zech. *3* (Enoch *40.* 7).
They tempt, they accuse, they punish, and they are the
servants of Satan himself.   Satan has no longer anything
to do with heaven.   He was banished from glory (cf. Life
of Adam and Eve *17.* 1) and he caused Adam and Eve to
be expelled from the joy and luxury of the Garden of Eden,
just as he himself had been driven out from joy and glory.

There is a reference to Satan in Ecclesiasticus *21.* 27 :
'when the ungodly curseth Satan, he curseth his own

soul,' a passage which seeks apparently to prevent men from shifting from themselves the responsibility of their own wrong-doing. Satan is the arch-tempter, but this does not absolve the individual from the guilt of sin. According to Wisdom of Solomon (*2*. 24), it was through the enmity of the devil (*diabolos*) that death entered into the world. Here we can trace the beginning of that tendency by which the serpent of the Garden of Eden comes to be identified with the devil. The idea of the Satan-serpent becomes more and more common after this, perhaps because of this same identification in the Persian system. The synthesis is found in the Secrets of Enoch, in the Targums and the Midrashes, and in Christian tradition generally. This latter is plainly set forth in Rev. *12*. 9, where we find a general equation embracing many different elements: 'and the great dragon was cast down, the old serpent, he that is called the Devil and Satan, the deceiver of the whole world'. See also the similar passage in Rev. *20*. 2. Another passage of the same type is to be found in the Apocalypse of Moses *17*. 1–4: 'Satan appeared in the form of an angel (cf. 2 Cor. *11*. 14) and sang hymns like angels', and he spake through the mouth of the serpent tempting Eve.

In *Tobit* (*c*. 200 B.C.) the name of the evil spirit is Asmodæus (*3*. 8, 17). There can be little doubt but that this name has its origin in ancient Persian religion, where the name of the evil demon is *Æshma dæva*, that is 'lustful demon', especially since in Tobit *3*. 8 it is clear that the slaying of the seven husbands is connected with the lust of the demon, who evidently desired himself to lie with Sarah, destined to be wife to Tobit's son (*3*. 17). But the Hebrews, regarding the two words as one, seem to have connected the name with the root *shamad* (destroy). We thus get the title 'the destroyer' in Wisdom of Solomon *18*. 25, and from this the *apolluon* (Apollyon) of Rev. *9*. 11. In this last instance the word is connected with the Hebrew *'abaddon*, the place of the lost, that vast roomy emptiness which the older ideas held to extend, none knew how far or how deep, below Sheol, cf. Job *28.* 22 (English 'destruction' for the Hebrew *'abaddon*). Later Jewish lore makes Asmodæus king of all the demons with Lilith as their queen. It was, for instance, Asmodæus who enticed Noah into drunkenness. The legends also say that he took the form and throne of Solomon for a while, and committed all those sins for which Solomon himself is held blameworthy and responsible.

Another variation in the traditions is the identification of Azazel (Lev. *16.* 7–28) with the great corrupting power in the world. In Enoch *10.* 4–8 (pre-Maccabæan), Raphael is commanded to bind Azazel hand and foot and to cast him into the darkness, because 'the whole earth has been corrupted through the works that were taught by Azazel: to him ascribe all sin' (verse 8).

The kingdom over which the Devil reigns has very many servants, demons whose task it is to lead men astray and to defeat God. These demons are responsible for every kind of sin in men. According to the *Book of Jubilees* the demons are 'malignant spirits' who were the children of the fallen angels (*10.* 3–9), 'created in order to destroy', corrupting, leading astray and destroying the wicked. Their chief is Mastema, i.e. 'Enmity', the word being taken from the Hebrew of Hosea *9.* 7 and 8. They are (Jub. *12.* 20) 'the evil spirits who have dominion over the thoughts of men's hearts', 'to do all manner of wrong and sin (*11.* 5) and all manner of transgression, to corrupt and destroy, and to shed blood upon the earth'. They were responsible for the making and worship of idols, molten images, graven images and 'unclean *simulacra*' (*11.* 4).

According to the *Testaments of the Twelve Patriarchs*, Reuben *3.* 3-6, there are seven spirits of deceit which 'are appointed against men, and they are leaders in the works of youth'. These are the spirits of fornication, greed, fighting, obsequiousness, pride, lying, injustice, and to these an eighth has been added, namely sleep (i.e. error and fantasy). Other spirits are mentioned elsewhere in the Testaments, jealousy (Judah *13*. 3), envy (Simeon *3*. 1; *4*. 7), anger (Dan. *2*. 4), etc. The Testaments as a whole have a developed demonology, with the chief named Beliar (Levi *3*. 3; etc.), the Prince of Deceit (Simeon *2*. 7), and the Devil (Naphtali *8*. 4). He rules over all who yield to their evil inclination (Asher *1*. 8), but he flees from the righteous who keep the Law (Dan. *5*. 1. Naphtali *8*. 4). Ultimately he will be bound (Levi *18*. 12), and cast into Gehenna (Judah *25*. 3). But the most extraordinary development is the statement that 'with all wickedness the spirits of wickedness work' in the tribe of Dan (Dan. *5*. 6). The following verse reads : 'For I have read in the book of Enoch the righteous that your prince is Satan'. It was Dan who led Levi astray, for this interpolation belongs to the first century B.C., and is in opposition to the Hasmonæan high-priestly kings who had thought more of military prowess than of the things pertaining to true religion. The condemnation of Dan is a development from the idolatry of Dan in the Old Testament, Judges *18*. 30. 1 Kings *12*. *29*. Presumably all this is why Dan is omitted from the list of the redeemed in Rev. *7*. 5-8.

The evil spirits are not left anonymous, for we find a whole hierarchy of them, and all the leaders named. These names appear in the *Book of Enoch* as those who once were angels in heaven, but saw the daughters of men that they were fair (Gen. *6*. 1-6). Their leader was Semjaza, and there were two hundred of them altogether, of whom the names of 'their chiefs of tens' are given in Enoch *6*. 7. There are nineteen altogether in the list, including Semjaza himself, and the twentieth is Azazel, who is, in some degree at least, as much the leader as Semjaza. Elsewhere these fallen angels are called 'the Watchers' (Enoch *10*. 7; *15*. 1-*16*. 4; *19*. 1-3. 2 Enoch *18*. 1-5; etc.). These will ultimately be cast down into Gehenna; cf. 2 Pet. *2*. *4*. Rev. *20*. 2f.

The origin of a belief in this type of evil spirit is mostly non-Israelitish. There are indications of a belief in demons or evil spirits which go back to the earliest times, part of 'the hole of the pit whence they were digged'. There are references to the *Se'irim* (hairy ones, R.V. 'he-goats') to whom sacrifices were made (Lev. *17*. 7. 2 Kings *23*. 8: where we should probably read *se'irim* 'hairy ones' for *she'arim* 'gates'), to the *Ẓiyyim* (dry ones), demons of the wastes (Jer. *50*. 39); and probably to the *Robetz* ('the one that croucheth at the door,' Gen. *4*. 7), which has its parallel in Rabitzu, the door-demon of the Babylonians. We find also references to such demons of human shape as *Lilith* the night-hag (R.V. 'night-monster') in Isa. *34*. 14: and '*Aluqah* (vampire: R.V. 'horseleach') in Prov. *30*. 15, who is a flesh-devouring ghoul of insatiable appetite.

It is nevertheless doubtful whether there is enough here to give rise in itself to the full-orbed demonology which envisages rank upon rank of evil spirits such as those which are under the charge of Azazel and Semjaza. It is true that, according to Jewish tradition, they have their origin in the Fallen Angels of Gen. *6*. 1–6, but there is definitely Persian influence to be seen in the graded ranks of the evil ones. According to the developed Persian system, the evil spirit Angra-Mainyu is the head of all the hosts of evil, and under him are six chief evil ones of whom the leader is Æshma (i.e. *Æshma dæva*, cf. Asmodæus.) Under these six chief demons there are between fifty and sixty other demons, the demons of pride, lust, sloth, and so forth, making up all the vices of human kind. Next under these is the whole host of evil spirits, those actual demons who bring all sorts of trouble and sorrow to men. It can scarcely be accidental that these ordered phalanxes of evil spirits are to be found in Jewish demonology as well as in Persian demonology. Evil spirits are commonly believed to exist amongst primitive peoples the whole world over, and often by peoples far from primitive. It is the grades of evil spirits that are so significant. There is no need to assume that the demons of disease are of Persian origin, even though Angra Mainyu, during his period of ascendancy in the third period of the world's history, did invent a hundred thousand diseases save one. The belief that every kind of sickness, from insanity downwards, is due to the demons is common throughout the world.

We have dealt hitherto with the demonology of later Judaism. There is also a highly developed angelology, with a similar difference between native Hebrew ideas and the later ordered hierarchy of holy ones.

We pass by the use of the phrase 'the angel of the Lord' as an expression to denote a temporary manifestation of God, a theophany. The phrase is found in such passages as Gen. *16.* 7–14; etc., (J), and in the E tradition in the form 'the angel of God', Gen *21.* 17–19; etc. There are many instances in even the earliest strata of the Old Testament of angels thought of as heavenly beings distinct from God Himself, e.g. the 'angels of God' whom Jacob saw in his dream at Bethel 'ascending and descending' the ladder set up on the earth, whose top reached to heaven (Gen. *28.* 12). There were angels who were guests of Abraham, though so like men that he entertained angels unawares (Gen. *18.* 8). We have already made reference to 'the sons of God', amongst whom was the Satan, who formed the heavenly court in Job *1.* 6. With these there is to be reckoned the verse in Job (*38.* 7) which, in telling of the joy of the Creation, refers to the occasion 'when the morning stars sang together, and all the sons of God shouted for joy'. Elsewhere, e.g. in Isa. *6*, the heavenly court is composed of *Seraphim*. These creatures are winged, as also are the living creatures of Ezekiel's vision (Ezek. *1.* 4; etc.), but there is no particular indication of this elsewhere in the Old Testament, though Philo describes them as having wings, and we find them so in the New Testament (Rev. *14*. 6). It may be that their wings are taken for granted to a greater extent than the silence would warrant, though they generally appear in human form, and are called men in Gen. *18*. 2, 16 and in other cases. This is the case even in Dan. *9*. 21, 'the man Gabriel', though in this book heavenly beings are represented as human beings, and earthly beings are represented as beasts. The angels are not called 'spirits' in the Old Testament, for the phrase, 'He maketh his angels spirits' should be rendered, 'He maketh the winds his messengers', Ps. *104*. 4. The Hebrew *ruach* means both 'wind' and 'spirit', and *mal'ak* (like the Greek *angelos*) means 'messenger' primarily, and 'angel' only secondarily.

It is probable that there was a double* origin of the *Seraphim* and of the *Cherubim*. There are the seraphim who are serpent-demons of the waste places, but there are also the heavenly seraphim who are personifications of the lightnings. Similarly there are the winged cherubs whose prototypes are to be seen in the winged figures of Babylon, the guardian-spirits of their mythology (cf. Gen. *3*. 24), and also the twin cherubs who are personifications of the twin spirits of the thunder (cf. the Heavenly Twins, *Dioscuri*, Castor and Pollux).

With the return from the Exile developments are manifest. We have seen that the Satan gradually deteriorated until he became the king of the counter-kingdom of evil. We also find the gradual development of ranks of angels in descending order of importance and authority, and all of it comparable to the range of evil spirits which we have found in the *Book of Enoch* and elsewhere. It is stated in the Genesis Midrash (*Bereshith Rabba*) *48*, and again in the Jerusalem Talmud (*Rosh hash Shanah 1*. 2) that 'the names of the angels were brought by the Jews from Babylonia'.

---

* See OESTERLEY AND ROBINSON: *Hebrew Religion* (second edition, 1937), pp. 111f, 291f, where in each case a single origin is proposed.

This means that such nomenclature is post-exilic, but not necessarily that it was Babylonian in origin. It was doubtless Persian in origin, just as the names of the demons and their grades are Persian in origin.

In the *Book of Daniel* we have the idea of the 'princes' ('captains', the word being the same as that in Joshua 5. 15, 'the captain of the host of the Lord'), who are national patron angels. Michael is 'one of the first captains' (R.V. 'one of the chief princes') and the guardian angel of Israel, Dan. *10*. 13; *12*. 1. He has been contending with 'the prince of Persia', and he must return to contend with him again and also with 'the prince of Greece', *10*. 13, 20. In the New Testament, in Jude 9, he is Michael the archangel, and this represents a further development (cf. 1 Thess. *4*. 16). There is another angelic figure mentioned in Dan. *8*. 16; *9*. 21: 'the man Gabriel', who elsewhere is one of the seven archangels. In Ezek. 9 there are in all seven angels, an angel with an inkhorn and six destroyers. The angel with the inkhorn is a picture of the Babylonian god, Nebo (Nabu), the scribe of the gods, who is regularly represented with the inkhorn at his girdle. He is the origin of the Recording Angel of popular Christian angelology. Here, for the first time, we find a group of seven, though it is rather six plus one.

It is often stated that the seven archangels have their origin in the 'immortal holy ones', the Amesha Spenta (Amashaspands) of the Zoroastrian system, but this assumption is due to a misapprehension. There are not seven, but six, and the number can be made into seven only by the inclusion of Ahura Mazda himself. It is claimed that in later Zoroastrianism there were indeed seven Amashaspands, but this total is probably due to Semitic influence and not vice versa. It is more likely that the seven archangels are to be traced, in so far as the number seven is concerned, to Babylonian influence, with its major seven 'stars', i.e. the sun, moon and five planets.

A third angel appears in the *Book of Tobit*, Raphael by name (*3*. 17), and he is described later in the book (*12*. 15) as 'one of the seven holy angels'. The 'seven' is the ancient magic number which crops up again and again in magico-religious associations. We find it in the seven-day taboos of the Assyrian system, sacred days on which almost every kind of activity was prohibited. It is found in the seven locks of Samson's hair which gave him supernatural strength (Judges *16*. 19), in the seven lookings for the storm cloud by Elijah's servant (1 Kings *18*. 44), and so on in-numerably. Each period of passage in the human life is a seven-day period; seven days of birth with circumcision on the eighth day, seven days of marriage, and seven days of mourning for the dead. There is therefore not the slightest need to look away to the six Amashaspands plus Ahura Mazda for the origin of the seven holy angels.

We have seen that, in the *Book of Tobit*, reference is made to Raphael as 'one of the seven holy angels' (*12*. 15). Their task is 'to present the prayers of the saints, and to go in before the glory of the Holy One'. In Enoch *20*. 1–7, we find the names of the seven 'holy angels who watch'. They are Uriel, Raphael, Raguel, Michael, Saraqael, Gabriel, and Remiel. But the number seven is by no means firm. Zechariah (*1*. 20: Hebrew *2*. 3) saw four heavenly smiths in his vision whose duty it was to cast down the four horns which had scattered Judah, Israel, and Jerusalem. This 'four' appears again in Enoch *40*. 1–10 (*Similitudes*, first half of first century B.C.), where we read of 'four presences who utter praises before the Lord of Glory'. Their names are Michael, Raphael, Gabriel, and Phanuel. These are the four presences 'on the four sides of the Lord of Spirits' (*40*. 2), and are probably a develop-ment from the vision of the chariot-throne of God in Ezek. *1*. This is clear from Enoch *71*. 7–13, where closest to the throne are these four angels of the Presence, 'and round about were Seraphim, Cherubim, and Ophannim', with 'angels who could not be counted, a thousand thousands, and ten thousand times ten thousand encircling that house'. The Ophannim (wheels) are personifications of the wheels of the chariot-throne, 'for the spirit of the living creature was in the wheels' (Ezek. *1.* 21; cf. *10.* 17). Later the Eyes ('*Enim*) and the Living Creatures (*Chayyoth*) also came to be regarded as angels. In the *Apocalypse of Moses* (*40.* 1: in the C text, Tischendorf's third Vienna MS.), the names of the four archangels appear as Michael, Gabriel, Uriel, and Raphael. Both traditions are combined in Rev. *4.* 5, 6, etc., in the four living creatures (A.V. unfortunately 'beasts') and the seven spirits.

We have said that there is no connection between the seven archangels of Jewish lore and the six Amashaspands of Zoroastrianism, the later 'seven' there being due probably to Jewish-Semitic influence rather than otherwise. Neither is there any discernible connection between the names, for the names of the Amashaspands are Asha, Vohu mano, Khshathra, Armaiti, Haurvatat, and Ameretat. The names of the Jewish 'holy ones' show that they are personifications or hypostasisations of various characteristics of the Divine Nature, or of the various activities of God. For instance, Michael means 'Who is like God' and so expresses His transcendence. Gabriel means 'Man of El', or perhaps 'Mighty one of El', to express His might. On the other hand the Amashaspands are personifications of ideas such as Law, the good disposition and so forth, though some allege that this is a later development, and that they were originally personifications of natural forces or elemental powers of Nature. This is similar to the kind of thing we find in Enoch *60.* 11–24, where angels are allocated to the elements, e.g. the spirit of the sea, and so forth. It is said (verse 17) that 'the spirit of the hoar-frost is his own angel, and the spirit of the hail is a good angel'. Then it is said that the spirit of the snow has forsaken his chamber on account of his strength, but that there is a

special spirit therein, and its name is frost.   And so on, for
mist, dew, rain, and lastly, 'the angel of peace'.   Or
again, in Jubilees *2*. 2, we read of the creation in the
beginning of 'the angels of the spirit of fire and the angels
of the spirit of the winds, and the angels of the spirits of
the clouds, and of darkness . . .', and also snow, hail, hoar-
frost, etc., much as in Enoch *60*.   From this it is natural to
read in Jubilees *35*. 17 that there are guardian angels, not
only for the various kinds of weather, but also for individuals; cf. Matt. *18*. 10.   There is an analogy here with
the *Fravashis* of Zoroastrianism, 'the powerful pre-eminent
guardian-angels of the true believers' (Yasht *13*. 1).

CHAPTER XIV

THE LAW

THE Hebrew word for the Law is *Torah*. It means 'instruction, direction'. It is usually rendered by the English word 'law', but such a translation is wholly inadequate, and has proved to be altogether misleading. The rendering is due, in the first place, to the Septuagint rendering, *nomos*. The influence of this is to be seen in all the subsequent versions. In point of fact, the word *torah* includes everything that God has made known, whether by priest, prophet, or psalmist.

The primary reference is to God, and to recognise this is essential to any proper understanding of the real meaning of the word. The lexicon* gives instances first of human direction, and then of divine direction. This is wrong, and is indicative of the whole modern approach to the study of religion. The word *torah* meant divine direction before it was used for human direction. The 'human' uses of the word are all, with the sole exception of Ps. *78*. 1, to be found in *Proverbs* (thirteen times). This use is an instance of the kind of thing which often happens in the development of words, whereby the original significance becomes blurred and lost. The word originally had to do with divine direction as distinct from and even as against human direction.

When an Israelite went to a shrine to ask for a definite ruling on some particular matter of belief or conduct it

* i.e. the *Oxford Hebrew-English Lexicon,* by Brown, Driver and Briggs.

was the duty of the priest to give that ruling. If the
question had been asked before, or if for any reason the
priest knew the answer, then he would give the ruling.
It would be an answer according to precedent, and it was
called a *mishpat*, a word which is usually translated 'judgement' in the Old Testament, but can sometimes be translated 'manner' (Judges *18.* 7; etc.).

If, however, the question was new, so that there was no
precedent, then the priest would have to consult the
Oracle. He might do this by sacrifice, being careful to
examine the liver of the victim.*   More probably he would
cast the sacred lot. The logic of this is: there are no uncaused events; an event uncaused by human agency is
therefore caused by non-human agency. When, therefore, the priest of Jehovah casts the lot, the fall of the 'dice'
is directed by Jehovah. The sacred lot was by *Urim* and
Thummim (cf. the Septuagint of 1 Sam. *14.* 41. Also
Ezra *2.* 63. Neh. *7.* 65). These were possibly two small
images (so Philo), or, more likely, two differently coloured
stones (so Driver), one of which, probably *Thummim*,
signified 'Yes', and the other, *Urim*, signified 'No'. The
lot was cast (Hebrew *yarah*), and so the *torah* (a noun
derived from the verb *yarah*) was given. The *torah* was
thus a direct answer given by God. The word was
extended, equally with the other word *mishpat* (judgement,
precedent) to apply also to oracles given by the prophet,
whether according to precedent, or through dream, vision,
and ecstasy. Originally, however, both words seem to
have been connected with the function of the priest, so
that in Deut. *33.* 10 the function of Levi is described as
teaching 'Jacob thy judgements (*mishpat*) and Israel thy
law (*torah*)'.

---

* Cf. the Gezer 'liver tablet' of hard-baked clay and covered with
cross-lines. See S. A. COOK: *The Religion of Ancient Palestine in the
Light of Archaeology* (Schweich Lectures, 1925), p. 103; also the fac-
simile at the end of the book, Plate xxiii, fig. 2.

The next stage is that the word comes to be used for the whole body of prophetic teaching (e.g. Jer. *9*. 13), or again of the general priestly instruction in relation to sacred things (e.g. Hos. *4*. 6). A further development is in connection with the written Deuteronomic Law, so that we find the phrase, growing more and more common, 'the scroll of the law' (Deut. *28*. 61). When this phrase occurs in *Chronicles*, it may be presumed to stand for the whole of the Law, including the Priestly Code, i.e. for substantially the whole Law of Moses as it is found in the Pentateuch.

This written Law was the foundation of post-exilic Jewry, and it may be dated as roughly about 400 B.C. It was, however, only the foundation, for developing Jewry demanded guidance in respect of the new problems which necessarily arose as the years passed by. Thus there arose a body of Oral Tradition, and this in time grew to be regarded as at least as binding as the written Law itself. This was only to be expected. If the rigid keeping of the Law of Moses was to be the duty and delight of the Jew, then it is clear that the Oral Tradition was bound to be of paramount importance, because this told the Jew how to apply the written Law in his daily life. It was by the Oral Tradition that he knew how to apply the age-old precepts in a world of new ideas and alien customs. Without the Oral Tradition, the pious Jew would not know what to do on the ever-growing number of occasions when he could not find an exact parallel in the ancient scrolls.

Further, post-exilic Jewry was dominantly separatist in its policy. This separatism developed to no small degree around the keeping of the Sabbath and the careful discrimination between the clean and the unclean. Such separatist behaviour involved the strictest observance of the Law in its minutest details. These were the things which kept the Jew separate from the heathen in the midst of a

heathen world. It was of the utmost importance that in
any particular line of conduct he should know exactly
where he was from the start, lest perchance he found himself unwittingly involved in the customs of the heathen.
Every endeavour was therefore made on this ground also
to ensure accurate pronouncements as to how the Law was
actually to be observed. The salvation of the Jew depended
upon his exact observance of the Law. Whilst, therefore,
it is true that the word *torah* has a much wider application
than our word 'law', it is nevertheless the case that it
was associated chiefly with details of conduct, and it
was inevitable that it should tend to take on a legal
aspect.

We have already seen something of the growing importance of the observance of the Law in the *Book of Ezra-
Nehemiah.* This appears as early as Nehemiah's prayer in
Neh. *1.* 7. The non-observance of the Law is there
regarded as having been the cause of all Israel's woes.
The same attitude is to be seen in Neh. *9.* 14, 29, 34. The
connection of Nehemiah's separatist policy and the Law of
Moses is to be seen chiefly in Neh. *13.* 1–3. The climax,
when the Law was formally established as the guide and
rule of daily life, is to be found in Neh. *8.* Ezra the scribe
brings the Law before the congregation, and reads it to
them, both men and women. Already in this description
we have evidence of a liturgy connected with the reading
of the Law. When Ezra opened the book (verse 2), all
the people stood. Then there followed a benediction, to
which the people replied, 'Amen, Amen', and bowed their
heads, prostrating themselves to the ground. The Law
was then read, and whilst the people still stood, the
interpreters made sure that they understood (verses
7 and 8). This was the beginning of the regular system in
the synagogues whereby the reading of the Law was
followed by a rendering of the passage into the vernacular
Aramaic.

Further development in the importance of the Law is to be seen in two pre-Maccabæan books, the *Wisdom of Ben-Sira** (Ecclesiasticus) and the *Book of Tobit*; and also, as we hold, in the first Psalm. Both books belong to the years immediately following the beginning of the second century B.C., and it is possible that the first Psalm is as late as any in the Psalter.

The growing importance of the functions of the scribe, i.e. the man who is learned in the Law, is to be seen in Ecclus. *38. 24-39.* 11. In the first part of this section, up to the end of chapter *38*, we have an admirable description of the work of those 'who maintain the fabric of the world', but have no opportunity to become wise. For 'the wisdom of the scribe cometh by opportunity of leisure, and he that hath little business shall become wise'. Then, in chapter *39*, we have Ben-Sira's famous eulogy of the scribe. He it is (*38.* 33) who shall 'be sought for in the council of the people', 'shall declare instruction and judgement', i.e. *torah* and *mishpat*. We thus see that the scribe has taken over the duty which once was pre-eminently the priest's. He it is who now gives decisions from God concerning practice and belief. He is the man on whom now chiefly depends men's understanding and proper observance of that Law which has come to be the guide of national and personal life. Ben-Sira is a conservative in all these matters, and he deprecates a too-modern interpretation of the Law. In the original text of Ecclus. *32:* 17, he says that 'the man of violence concealeth instruction, and forceth the Law to his necessity'. It has been thought that this couplet may represent an attitude unsympathetic to men like the Chasidim, those men, wholly devoted to the Law, who later resorted to arms in defence of it, and formed the backbone of the resistance in the time of the Maccabees. It is more likely that he is deprecating the

* The Greek spelling is Sirach, the —ch being added to make the word undeclinable.

development of Oral Tradition, a matter to which we must revert presently.

Ben-Sira holds that all a man's converse should be in the Law of the Most High (*9.* 15), and in *32.* 24, he equates 'trusting in Jehovah' with 'observing the Law'. To transgress the commandment is despicable (*10.* 19). The man who hates the Law is not wise, and is 'tossed about like a ship in a storm'.* Ben-Sira then goes on to compare discerning the Law to the ancient custom of seeking the oracle (*Urim*), an unexpected confirmation of the connection between *torah* and the casting of the sacred lot.

Yet, for all his insistence on the importance of keeping the Law, Ben-Sirah is no legalist. Sacrifice in itself is of no avail : 'The sacrifice of the unrighteous man is a mocking offering, and unacceptable are the oblations of the godless. The Most High hath no pleasure in the offerings of the ungodly, neither doth He forgive sins for a multitude of sacrifices' (*34.* 18, 19). At the end of the same chapter he says, 'Even so, a man fasting for his sins, and again doing the same—who will listen to his prayer? And what hath he gained by his humiliation?' He regards the Oral Tradition as of the utmost importance (*8.* 9) : 'Reject not the tradition of the aged, which they heard from their fathers', but he certainly did not fail to attach at least as much importance to the inward Law that was written on the heart.

Another important element in the teaching of Ben-Sira is the way in which he brings the Wisdom teaching of post-exilic Jewry within the orbit of the study of the Law. There was probably a time when the Wisdom teaching of the Jews might have developed into a philosophy after the pattern of the Greeks, but the Hebrew tendency to think in practical rather than in theoretical terms pre-

* See the critical text by R. H. CHARLES: *Apocrypha and Pseudepigrapha of the Old Testament*, Vol. I.

vented this. The great and growing importance of the
Law, with its stress on certain things which must actually
be done, was also effective in this respect. We can see the
process at work in the writings of Ben-Sira. There was
always a strong element of worldly wisdom in the Wisdom
of the Jews, and this wisdom in affairs combined easily
with the emphasis on the doing of the Law. The two
streams blend. This is to be seen in Ecclus. *15* and in *24*,
where (verse 23) it is definitely stated that all the things
which pertain to Wisdom are to be found in the Law. A
parallel is drawn between the blessings of Wisdom and the
fulness of the four rivers of Paradise. Equally clear is the
statement of *19..20*, where he states that 'all wisdom is the
fear of the Lord, and all wisdom is the fulfilling of the
Law'. The development here can be seen by comparison
with the verse in the *Book of Job* (*28.* 28) on which this
saying is modelled: 'Behold, the fear of the Lord, that is
wisdom; and to depart from evil is understanding'.

Ben-Sira emphasises the study of the Law, as befits a
man of his evident temperament, though he is anxious
enough to see it all translated into practice. The more
practical emphasis, however, is to be found in the *Book of
Tobit*. Here we see the Law already established as the
rule of daily life. The going up to Jerusalem to keep the
feasts is an ordinance 'unto all Israel by an everlasting
decree' (*1.* 6), and the same applies to tithes and first-
fruits. References to these institutions of Jewry are to be
found again in *2.* 1; *5.* 13. Restrictions as to marriage
are such as are determined by the Law of Moses (*6.* 12;
7. 13), whilst the influence of *Deuteronomy* is to be seen in
4. 5f. There is a strong emphasis on almsgiving (*4.* 8–10;
12. 8), and emphasis on fasting also (*12.* 8). All these
matters are those which came to be regarded as of paramount importance during the next two centuries, as even a
slight acquaintance with the Gospels will show.

In Psalm *1* we find a strong emphasis on the study of the

Law. The happy man is the man whose 'delight is in the Law of the Lord, and in His Law doth he meditate day and night' (verse 2). As we have said, this psalm is probably one of the latest psalms in the book, and was inserted in its present position at the time when the Psalter was arranged to be read according to a triennial system, parallel with the Palestinian triennial lectionary for the Reading of the Law. The psalmist has borrowed part of the picture in Jer. *17*. 8, but for him 'trusting in the Lord' has become 'meditating in the Law', just as, in Ecclus. *32*. 24, 'trusting in the Lord' is equated with 'observing the Law'. It is quite possible that no great distance of time intervened between Psalm *1* and Ben-Sira.

Next in order is the *First Book of the Maccabees*, written under the influence of the great fight for the religion and the Law which began when Mattathias cut down the Greek officer at Modein. The beginning of the troubles is detailed in 1 Macc. *1*. 11–15, where a party within Jewry is charged with making terms with the Gentile civilisation. Their following of Greek customs, especially their 'making themselves uncircumcised', is the equivalent of 'forsaking the holy covenant'. All these Hellenising Jews are 'transgressors of the Law'. It is plain that a number of Jews were revolting against the separatist policy which had been dominant from the time of Ezra onwards, and it is plain also that the cutting edge of the separatist policy was the strict observance of the Law.

The insistent attempt of Antiochus Epiphanes to wipe out the Jewish religion and to destroy every copy of the Law did a very great deal to ensure a more rigid determination to hold on to these things. Opposition from Hellenisers within Jewry did but increase the resistance of the faithful. So determined were they to observe the Law in all its strictness that they even refused to defend themselves on the Sabbath, with the result that many of them were massacred, and their women and children with them (1 Macc. 2. 32f).* That this was no new fanaticism is to be seen from a similar incident which took place in the early years after the death of Alexander, when, in 321 B.C., the Jews stubbornly refused to defend themselves against Ptolemy I and were carried captive into Egypt.

We find a strong insistence on the observance of the Law in the *Book of Judith*. This book goes back to the middle of the second century B.C., but the existing Greek text is not later than the beginning of the first century A.D. We therefore cannot be sure to what extent it represents earlier opinion. Judith is the type of the faithful Jewess. She was very rich, for her husband, Manasses, had left her large monies and properties, but she was so strict in her mourning for him that, apart from the joyful festivals (e.g., the Sabbath, when no mourning was permitted), she dwelt in a tent on the roof of her house, dressed in sackcloth, and this during the whole of her widowhood of three years and four months. She observed all the feasts and joyful days, including not only the sabbaths and the new moons, but even the eves of the sabbaths and the new moons (*8. 6*). This observance of the eves of festivals is sound according to the rules in the Talmud.

Judith did more than was required according to the strict letter of the Law. This was part of a movement towards the rabbinic ideal of 'setting a fence about the Law' in order to guard against even an inadvertent infringement. Examples are to be found in the Mishnah, on the very first page.† According to Lev. 7. 15; 22. 30, nothing of the peace-offering or of the sacrifice of thanksgiving may be left till the morning. The rabbinic instruction in the Mishnah, *Ber. 1. 1*, is that all must be finished by midnight. Judith similarly begins to observe the festivals of sabbath and new moon on the eve.

* Cf. p. 38 above.
† So Moore points out in *Judaism*, Vol. I, p. 33.

This period following the Maccabæan wars was one of great rigour in the application of the Law. The *Book of Jubilees* belongs to this time, when the exact wording of scripture was emphasised with a fanatical exactness and interpreted with a strictness soon seen to be past bearing. The Talmud (*Sanh.* 46a) tells of a time when a man was put to death for riding on a horse (cf. Hos. *14*. 3). Cohabitation of husband and wife on the Sabbath was prohibited. Some men would have no intercourse with their wives from the close of the Sabbath to the fourth day of the week, lest their wives should bear children on the Sabbath, and so desecrate the Sabbath by doing something. Jubilees *50*. 6–13 contains very strict rules concerning the observance of the Sabbath, including the prohibition of cohabitation. In *49*. 20 it is commanded that the passover should be eaten 'in the court of the house which has been sanctified in the name of the Lord'. Charles was of the opinion* that this custom was actually observed, and that it had to be relaxed later because of the tremendous crowds which came up to the feast during the last days of the Temple. According to the Mishnah (*Sebach.* V, 8. *Makk.* III, 3) the passover could be eaten anywhere in Jerusalem, and this was certainly the custom followed by the Lord Jesus (Mark *14*. 12–16). It is more likely that the *Jubilees* regulation is an attempt to tighten up the prevailing custom in the interests of a strict interpretation of scripture, e.g. of Deut. *16*. 7: 'thou shalt eat it in the place which the Lord thy God shall choose' being interpreted to mean in the very court of the Temple itself. There are other details which are very strict—for instance, Jubilees *21*. 12f, where the kind of wood to be used on the altar is specified. There is no restriction laid down in the written Law, but *Jubilees* allows twelve kinds—cypress, bay, almond, fir, pine, cedar, savin (a kind of fir, or, perhaps, juniper), fig, olive, myrrh, laurel,

* *Apocrypha and Pseudepigrapha*, Vol. II, p. 81, note.

and aspalathus (some kind of prickly shrub). The Mishnah, however, allows all kinds of wood except vine and olive (*Tamid* II, 3), probably because these two are important for food. Once again, it is probable that in *Jubilees* we have an attempt to impose stricter regulations in a time of intense fanaticism. Another instance is to be found in Jubilees *49*. 1, where the passover lamb is required to be slain 'before it was even' instead of 'between the two evenings'. (Ex. *12*. 6).

The *Book of Jubilees* exalts the Law to the very heavens themselves. It was prescribed on the heavenly tablets (*3*. 31; *6*. 17, 29, etc.). The Sabbath is kept in heaven by the two foremost ranks of angels, 'all the angels of the presence, and all the angels of sanctification, these two great classes' (*2*. 18). These have been bidden to keep the Sabbath with God. They 'kept the Sabbath in the heavens before it was made known to any flesh to keep Sabbath thereon on the earth' (*2*. 30). No other angels and no other people are permitted to keep the Sabbath, because 'this law and testimony was given to the children of Israel as a law for ever unto their generations' (*2*. 33).

The attitude of the Jew who lived amongst the Gentiles during the last quarter of the second century B.C. was very different. It is illustrated in 2 Macc. *3*. 3f: 'But the Jews (those that dwelt in Alexandria) continued to maintain their goodwill towards the kings, and their unswerving fidelity. Yet, worshipping God and living according to His law, they held themselves apart in the matter of food; and for this reason they were disliked by some; but adorning their conversation by the good practice of righteousness they were established in the good report of all.'

This carefulness in observing the Law without an accompanying belligerence towards the Gentiles is to be seen in the *History of Susannah*, of whom it is said (vv. 2, 3) that she was 'a very fair woman, and one that feared the Lord', for 'her parents were righteous and taught their daughter according to the Law of Moses'. Or again, in the latest portions of *Enoch*, there is no insistence on carrying out the strictest details of the Law, but a general demand to do the commandments (verse 4) and not to 'transgress the eternal Law'.

In the *Testaments of the Twelve Patriarchs* (Levi *14*. 4), the Law is very far from being a means of separating Jew from Gentile. 'The light of the law was given for to lighten every man,' and the Jew is urged to keep the Law, if only for the sake of the Gentiles, for 'if ye be darkened through transgressions, what, then, will all the Gentiles do, living in blindness?' This particular passage probably belongs to the opening years of the first century B.C., and represents a warm-heartedness towards the Gentiles which maintained the hope of the salvation of the Gentiles with a strong universalism that was strangely alien to the larger body of opinion.

The climax in the exaltation of the Law is to be found in the *Apocalypse of Baruch*,* which belongs to the last years of the first century A.D. The whole book breathes a tremendous confidence in the destiny of Israel as the people who have been given the Law and have faithfully observed it. 'For we are all one celebrated people, who have received one Law from One; and the Law which is amongst us will aid us, and the surpassing wisdom which is in us will help us' (*48*. 24). The Law is the one possession which has been left to Israel apart from the Mighty One Himself: 'But now the righteous have been gathered, And the prophets have fallen asleep, And we also have gone forth from the land, And Zion hath been taken from us, And we have nothing now save the Mighty One and His Law' (*85*. 3). So long as Israel observes the Law, all will be well (*77*. 15; *44*. 7; *46*. 4). They will never lack lamp, or shepherd, or fountain (*77*. 16). If they remember it

---

* The Syriac *Apocalypse of Baruch*, sometimes cited as *2 Baruch*.

(*84*. 8), they will see the consolation of Zion (*44*. 7). On the other hand, 'justly do they perish who have not loved Thy Law, And torment of judgement shall await those who have not submitted themselves to Thy power' (*54*. 14).

But most of all we can see in this *Apocalypse of Baruch* that attitude to the Law against which the apostle, St. Paul, fought so resolutely. All the blessings of the world to come are promised to 'those who have been saved by their works, And to whom the Law hath now been a hope, and understanding an expectation, and wisdom a confidence' (*51*. 7). 'Those who have now been justified in My Law' will have their splendour glorified 'that they may be able to acquire and receive the world which doth not die, which is then promised to them' (*51*. 3). 'Hezekiah trusted in his works, and had hope in his righteousness' (*63*. 3), 'and the Mighty One heard him, for Hezekiah was wise, And He had respect unto his prayer, because he was righteous' (*63*. 5). Still further the good deeds and merits of the righteous are of avail for the people of God generally, and those of the patriarchs for their posterity (*2*. 2; *14*. 7; *84*. 10). Statements like these are precisely the kind of thing against which the Apostle Paul writes so vehemently (Rom. *3*. 20; etc.). Compare also St. Paul's 'passing away' of the Law (2 Cor. *3*. 7–11) with the 'eternal Law' (Baruch *59*. 2).

Belonging to the same period, but very different in attitude, is the *Ezra Apocalypse*, found in the *Apocrypha* in II Esdras *3–14*. The writer is equally sure that the Law can never pass away; 'the Law perisheth not, but remaineth in its honour' (*9*. 37). He does not regard the Law as having been instituted primarily for Israel, since God commanded all men 'what they should do to live, and what they should observe to avoid punishment' (*7*. 21). But the Gentiles refused His Law; they 'said moreover of the Most High, that he is not; and knew not his ways: but they despised his law, and denied his covenants; they have not been faithful to his statutes, and have not performed his works' (7. 22-24). And so God sowed His Law in Israel, that it might bring forth fruit in them, and that they might be glorified in it for ever (9. 30 f). And yet the Law is regarded as being inadequate for salvation. This is a remarkable statement for any first century A.D. Jew, and is astonishingly similar to words of St. Paul. The writer says: 'We that have received the Law shall perish by sin, and our heart also which received it' (9. 36). He further says that the disease of Adam was permanent. God did not take away from men their corrupt heart, so that his Law 'might bring forth fruit in them'. And yet the writer freely admits that we all 'have no works of righteousness', so that we all have great need of the divine mercy (8. 32). From this it may clearly be seen that we are but one step short of the position of the Apostle Paul. He, too, was in the same dilemma. The Law was, so the orthodox said, the Jew's one hope of salvation, and yet he himself was unable to fulfil the works demanded by the Law. The writer of the *Ezra Apocalypse* realises that the emphasis must be at least as much on the divine mercy as on the keeping of the Law. Paul goes the necessary step further, and says that ultimately it is all of the Divine mercy, or, as he would say, all is of grace, cf. Eph. 2. 5. Gal. 2. 16; etc.

There yet remains the matter of the Oral Tradition, the unwritten Law. We have seen that Ben-Sira regarded the Oral Tradition as of very great importance, when he bade men not to reject 'the tradition of the ages, which they heard from their fathers' (8. 9). We have also seen that some adjustments were essential if the Law was still to be applicable to the changing conditions of the centuries. The rabbis sought by every endeavour to make their *dicta* agree with that which the Law clearly ordained, and sought explicit scripture warrants. But sometimes no true scriptural warrant could be found for the rules of the rabbis. The custom was, in such a case, to say that it was 'a Mosaic rule from Sinai', that is, it was a rule given to Moses at the time when the written Law was held to have been instituted, but it was a rule which was not written down. The explanation was that in the days of mourning for Moses three thousand rules were forgotten, whilst Joshua forgot another three hundred.* These rules were not restored by either priest or prophet, but by the rabbis of later time.

There was one verse in the Law which might with justification have been a stumbling-block to the rabbis, namely Deut. *4.* 2: 'Ye shall not add unto the word which I command you, neither shall ye diminish from it', but Lev. *18.* 30 was interpreted to mean, 'Make an injunction additional to my injunction', and the way was clear. Then again Deut. *17.* 11 was interpreted to give authority to each generation to institute such rules as were judged to be necessary, while full advantage was taken of the somewhat peculiar† construction of Ps. *119.* 126. The usual rendering is: 'It is time for the Lord to work', but with a change of accent the line could be rendered: 'It is time to work for the Lord'. In this way warrant was found in an emergency for a regulation which was even contrary to the explicit teaching of the written Law.‡

Much of this was a development subsequent to the destruction of the Temple, and belonging to the second century A.D., but there are three notable cases in the first century A.D. where the plain teaching of the written Law was put aside. In one of these cases another passage of scripture was quoted. This case was the doing away of the ordeal of jealousy as prescribed in Num. *5.* 11–31. It

* Cf. MOORE: *Judaism* (1927), Vol. I, p. 256.

† Note the insertion of the *lamedh* after the infinitive construct. It is omitted in Kenn. MS. 76.

‡ MOORE: *Judaism*, I, pp. 259, 427; III, p. 80.

was during the period preceding the outbreak of the Jewish War of 66–70 A.D., when there was a serious decadence in public morality. Evidently there was so much adultery that the priests were overwhelmed by the number of charges brought. Rabbi Jochanan ben Zakkai thereupon abolished the ordeal, and found his justification in Hos. *4.* 14: 'I will not punish your daughters when they commit whoredom, nor your daughters-in-law when they commit adultery; for they themselves go apart with whores, and they sacrifice (i.e. eat sacred festival meals) with the temple-harlots.' The same passage* in the Mishnah tells of the abolition of the custom of Deut. *21.* 1–9 concerning the finding of a body in the open field. There were so many murders in those lawless days that it was not possible to follow the ancient rule. In this case, however, it was not possible to produce scriptural authority.

One of the most important of the rules of the rabbis which set at nought the Law was a device invented by Hillel. It was called *prosbul*, and it is obvious that something had to be done in this particular matter. It had to do with the Year of Release, the seventh year, when all debts were to be remitted (Deut. *15.* 1–18). It was an excellent piece of legislation in that it released the deserving poor from an encumbrance of debt, but it proved unworkable, for no man would lend money during the two years before the year of release, because of the risk that the loan would become a gift at the end of the period. And so Hillel devised a procedure by which the loan might be reclaimed at any time, independently of the Year of Release. In this way the whole intention of the humanitarian Deuteronomic Law was frustrated.

The authority of the Oral Tradition was found in the Great Synagogue. This was composed of pairs of rabbis, who handed on the tradition from generation to generation. Presumably there had to be two such teachers, since 'at

* Mishnah, *Sotah IX,* 9; cf. MOORE: *ibid.,* p. 260.

the mouth of two witnesses, or at the mouth of three witnesses, shall the matter be established' (Deut. *19*. 15). Whether there was actually such a 'Great Synagogue' is another matter, but some such device was necessary in order to afford authority to the Oral Tradition, which in course of time came to be regarded as of even greater importance than the written Law.

CHAPTER XV

WISDOM

WE saw in Chapter VIII (Part Two) that, during the Exile in Babylon, the Jews obtained a firm grasp of the fact that there is One God alone and none other but He. In those times the religion of the Jews became firmly and explicitly monotheistic. This transcendence of the One and Only God brought with it, in course of time, its own problem concerning contact between the Creator and the created, between God and man. There was not the slightest difficulty in the mind of the Second Isaiah himself, the prophet in whose writings these ideas are embodied. It is a remarkable fact that whilst no prophet is more sure of the uniqueness and the transcendence of God, there is no prophet more sure of His nearness. The prophet who could say: 'For as the heavens are higher than the earth, so are my ways higher than your ways, and my thoughts than your thoughts' (Isa. 55. 8, 9) is also the prophet who could say: 'When thou passest through the waters, I will be with thee; and through the rivers, they shall not overwhelm thee; when thou walkest through the fire, thou shalt not be burned; neither shall the flame kindle upon thee. For I am the Lord thy God, the Holy One of Israel, thy saviour' (43. 2f).

Succeeding generations, however, found a difficulty in bridging the gap between the holy God, far above all human thought, perfect in all His ways, and this rough earth with all its contrariness, including, most of all, man with all his waywardness and sin. We have seen how there developed a growing galaxy of angels, all graded according to ranks, from the Presences that surround the throne ultimately to ten thousand times ten thousand and tens of thousands. This development was mostly due to Persian (Iranian) influence, and it continued to develop long after the Persian Empire had crumbled before the onslaught of Alexander the Great in the latter half of the fourth century B.C.

It has been maintained by some scholars that there has been Persian influence at work also in the development of the figure of wisdom, as portrayed particularly in Prov. 8. On the other hand, some scholars have maintained that there is no Persian influence at all, and that this semi-personification of wisdom is a purely Jewish product. Whatever its origin, this much is certain, that the whole tendency arose out of an attempt to bridge the gap which seemed more and more to widen between God and the world, created by the growing ideas of the superlative excellence of God contrasted with this very mundane world below.

There is certainly a native Hebrew tradition of 'wisdom' (*chokmah*) stretching back into antiquity. It is found in such riddles as we find in the Samson story (Judges *14*. 14, 18), and in such proverbs as the saying about Nimrod the mighty hunter (Gen. *10*. 9), or that about Saul as a prophet (1 Sam. *10*. 12; *19*. 24). It is found also in the parable of Jotham (Judges *9*. 8–15) and in the later and more developed allegory-prophecy of Ezek. *31*. 1–9. Solomon's reputation for wisdom depended upon his aptitude for every kind of wise-saying, apophthegms, fables, parables and the rest (1 Kings *4*. 29–34), the kind of wordly wisdom and the clever expression of it which is appreciated all the world over, but nowhere more than amongst desert bedouin and their neighbours of old Palestine. The desert association of this type of gnomic wisdom is to be seen in the tradition which connects it with Edom (Jer. *49*. 7. Obad. *8*) and with 'the east'.

The setting of the *Book of Job*, for instance, is 'in the east', and the three friends apparently come from the Edomite country. Job is 'greatest of all the children of the east' (Job *1.* 3), and the perfect type of the wise and upright man.

To some degree the word *chokmah* (wisdom) runs parallel with the word *mana*, that more-than-human power which is described again and again in studies in primitive religion. Thus the word is used for the distinctive skill peculiar to any profession or occupation. It is used, for instance, of the skill needed for the making of the embroidered garments of the priests (Exod. *28.* 3), for the skill of the women in spinning the material for the holy garments (Exod. *35.* 25), in fact for every kind of skill, that of the soldier (Isa. *10.* 13), of the man of affairs (Gen. *41.* 39), and even of the magician (Exod. *7.* 11). In all these cases, and in many others which could be quoted, the word is used from a humanistic point of view. It is the special technical skill which can be seen in humankind. Inasmuch as such skill is regarded as more-than-human, it is thought of as being due to spirit-possession, and the word *ruach* (wind, breath, spirit) is used, the idea being that the doer is controlled by a super-human agency.

Chokmah is always concerned with what is done in this world. The worldly wisdom which is characteristic of the pithy sayings of the earliest period is always maintained. More and more, therefore, *chokmah* comes to mean that practical wisdom which enables a man to find happiness and prosperity in the conduct of his affairs. In this way it comes about that there is an association between wisdom and Law. The Hebrew knew that a man's truest wisdom lay in doing the will of God and in obeying His commandments. This association between wisdom and the Law is to be seen particularly from Deuteronomic times onwards, cf. Jer. *8.* 9; and almost everywhere in *Proverbs* and the wisdom literature generally.

In earlier times there had been three classes of men who proclaimed the word of God. The three classes are detailed in Jer. *18*. 18: 'For the law shall not perish from the priest, nor counsel from the wise, nor the word from the prophet,' though when the crash comes, something of this will indeed take place (Ezek. *7*. 26). In the days after the Exile, when the priest became more and more a sacrificing official and when prophecy declined, the wise men of Jewry assumed a growingly important position. The more the Law came to be regarded as the norm of daily life for every faithful Jew, the more the functions of the Wise Men and the Scribes (i.e. those who were learned in the Law) coincided, so that by the time we come to the second century B.C. the two classes are identified (Ecclus. *38*. 24; *39*. 1–11).

These Wise Men discussed the problems of life as they were created, for instance, by the rigid Deuteronomic principles of reward and retribution. The question of Job *14*. 14 is a typical problem for the Wise: 'If a man die, shall he live again?' Indeed the whole *Book of Job* is dealing with the problem of innocent suffering. Inasmuch, however, as the Wise Men addressed themselves to such human problems they came to take a less exclusive view than those who thought in terms of the Law. The Law was mainly separatist in its effect, and perhaps also in its intention. The wisdom of the Wise knew no such barriers. It tended to be international, so much so that Gressmann thought of a common origin for all the teachers, some central university from which, so to speak, they all graduated. But there is no need to posit anything so formal or exact as this. When men think of human problems they realise that these are common to all men of whatever race. There is no need, and indeed no opportunity, for exclusiveness in such realms. Philosophy, whether of Greece or of Zion, is international, just as is science of every type. The Law was definitely designed in the post-exilic period to set the Jew apart from the heathen. But when the Wise Men referred to the Law they naturally thought of it as being universal, and it is in their writings that the two coalesce.

Ben-Sira (second century B.C.) identifies the Law with wisdom. This is seen in *34*. 8: 'Without deceit shall the Law be fulfilled, And wisdom is perfect in a mouth that is faithful'*; or again: 'He that keepeth the Law controlleth his natural tendency, And the fear of the Lord is the consummation of wisdom' (*21*. 11). The statement in *19*. 20 is explicit: 'All wisdom is the fear of the Lord, and all wisdom is the fulfilling of the Law'.

There is another element in the teaching of Ben-Sira which has its roots in the personification, as some think, of wisdom in Prov. *8*. It is difficult to decide to what extent either Prov. *8*. or Ben-Sira is definitely personifying wisdom. It may be that both are speaking in poetical rhetorical terms, and that the apparent personification is due to this. Just as the man of affairs manages his affairs by *chokmah* (wisdom), so God, by wisdom, accomplished His creative work (Prov. *3*. 19). According to Ben-Sira, wisdom was created before the heavens and the earth (Ecclus. *1*. 4). The same sentiment is expressed in *24*. 9a, and both are clearly dependent on Prov. *8*. 22, 23. Now that we are dealing with a personification of wisdom, we find ourselves uncertain as to whether either the author of Prov. *8* or Ben-Sira regarded wisdom as being the instrument by which God created the world. Prov. *3*. 19 is different, and we judge that it means nothing more than we have indicated above, namely, God created the world by wisdom, just as the craftsman follows the work of his craft. But in the passages where wisdom is personified she seems to be a sympathetic onlooker rather than an active agent. Probably the writers were in each case careful in their restraint, realising that it is one thing to be

* The translation is that of Charles.

searching for an intermediary, and another thing to delegate to that intermediary such acts as would suggest that it also was a person distinct from God Himself.

We find, therefore, that there are limits to the personification of wisdom in both writers, and incline to the idea that here in the main we have a native Jewish product. On the other hand,* there are elements in the description of wisdom which do suggest that there is a certain amount of foreign influence. Attempts have been made to find an origin in Babylonian mythology (so Gressmann and Bohl), or in Egyptian lore, but, if there is indeed foreign influence, then the most likely origin is to be found in one of the six Amashaspands of the Zoroastrian system. Bousset† found the prototype in Armaiti, the 'immortal holy one' whom Plutarch identified with the Greek *Sophia* (Wisdom). The particular connection is in the special mention of 'the fear of the Lord' as being 'the beginning of wisdom', since Armaiti is said to be Piety. It is true that Armaiti is regarded as the inculcator of divine wisdom, but this is in relation to agricultural pursuits. There seems to be little connection between the two, apart from Plutarch's identification. There is more to be said for identification with Vohu mano, for Vohu mano is an intermediary in the work of Creation (Jasna, 31, 11), and stands for Good Intention (Plutarch, *eunoia*). But in respect of the part played in Creation the Hebrew *chokmah* stops short just where it ought to go forward, for we have seen that this is exactly where both the author of Prov. *8* and Ben-Sira hesitate. Rankin himself pleads for Asha as the prototype, and indeed there are many similarities of language and expression. It is Asha who is 'the embodiment of the world-order'. She has 'a beautiful dwelling place', and she urges men to choose the right as against a lie.

* For a full discussion of the pros and cons, see O. S. RANKIN: *Israel's Wisdom Literature* (Edinburgh, 1936), pp. 222–64.
† *Religion des Judentums*, p. 520.

No identification seems to us to be convincing, so that we judge the semi-personification of wisdom to be in the main a native Hebrew product, and an attempt within the limits of a strict monotheism to find an intermediary so that the pure and eternal God might have some association with this impure and ephemeral world.

Further development of the idea of wisdom, e.g. in the *Wisdom of Solomon*, is dependent rather upon the Greek idea of the *logos*, and this we discuss in the next chapter.

CHAPTER XVI

THE LOGOS

IN the search for some mediatory principle which might
fill the gap between the perfect God and this imperfect
world we must next consider influence from the philosophers
of the Greeks. This development is of the utmost importance. From the time of Alexander the Great onwards the
Jews were surrounded by Greek influences, both at the
hands of the Ptolemies of Egypt and at the instance of the
Seleucids of Antioch. In 1 Macc. *1.* 11, we have read
how many Israelites sought to 'make a covenant with the
Gentiles' and (verse 15) joined themselves to the Gentiles.
We have seen how the Jewish aristocracy were most anxious
to keep on good terms with their Gentile masters. Since
the idea of mediation and harmony is the essential characteristic of the whole Hellenist civilisation, it behoves us to
pay particular attention to this sphere of influence.

From our present point of view, Greek philosophy can
be regarded as the search for some unifying or mediating
principle in which (or in whom) 'all things hold together'
(Col. *1.* 17: *R.V. margin*). We can see how important this
search is for this aspect of our study (i.e. in connection with
the linking of God and the world together) by two passages
from Homer (*Iliad* xiv, 246 and 201), where the poet says
that Ocean is 'the origin (*genesis*, generating cause) of all'
and is also 'the *genesis* of the gods'. This myth was
rationalised by Thales (640–550 B.C.) in his statement that
water is the origin of all. Anaximander used the word
arche (beginning, first cause) and said that the *arche* was

to apeiron, the indeterminate and all-pervading 'stuff'.*
Perhaps *to apeiron* goes back to the Chaos of Hesiod
(*c.* 750 B.C.?), though it is probable that Hesiod meant
'space' rather than 'indeterminate stuff', for the passage
in Hesiod (*Theogony* 116) ought not to be interpreted in
accordance with the 'wasteness and voidness' of Gen. *1.* 2.
Anaximenes (*c.* 520 B.C.) made Air his *Arche*, whilst Herakleitos (Heraclitus) is said to have thought of the primeval
'stuff' as Fire.

The tendency of these pre-Socratic philosophers is,
with varying degrees of unprecision, to identify the *Arche*
with God. Thales says that 'all things are full of god'.
Anaximander says that the Infinite out of which all things
are produced is divine. Anaximenes calls his *Arche* (Air)
God, whilst Herakleitos, if this 'Dark One' is rightly
understood, thought of his primeval 'stuff' (his *Arche*) as
being God, but that part of it which was in the human
body was the soul. They all talk of a primeval 'substance', and yet they regard the universe as being alive.
From Anaximander onwards we find the idea of eternal
movement due to the strife between opposites. Herakleitos, for instance, says that 'war is the father of all' and
that things 'came to be through strife'. They are all
searching for something behind and within all things which
is solid and secure, and at the same time for some explanation of the transitoriness of things.

It is in Herakleitos that we get the first clear adum-
brations of the *Logos* idea, that idea which, thanks to the
activities of the Stoic philosophers, came to be the dominant
theme of the two centuries which mark the end of the pre-
Christian era and the beginning of the Christian era. To
Herakleitos everything is in a state of flux, and nothing
anywhere continues in one state. All permanence is an

---

* It is better to use the word 'stuff', since the word 'matter' has
come to have a meaning with us which it certainly could never have
had with Anaximander or any of the pre-Socratic philosophers.

illusion. But he did posit an innermost essence of things, the constant inevitable change, and this, he said, is analogous to reason in human beings. It is not necessarily self-conscious, neither is it purposeful, but it is orderly, an eternal process of change.

Parmenides, on the other hand, flatly denied this position of Herakleitos, and said that it was the change which was illusory, but when he comes to explain away the apparent change, he falls back on the idea of the strife of opposites, handed on by Pythagoras from Anaximander. Everything is harmonised by Eros ('love'), which Hesiod (*Theogony* 120) had declared to be the finest (*kallistos*, 'most beautiful'?) amongst the deathless gods.

The situation began to clear from its confusion in Empedokles, who posited four 'elements' (original 'substances'), Earth, Water, Air, and Fire. These four are for ever permanent, and the change that is obvious in the world comes from their changing relationships, but all is controlled by Love and Hate, the one being that which draws opposites together, and the other that which drives them apart.

Anaxagoras (born *c.* 500 B.C.) posited an indefinite number of elements, all controlled by *Nous*, pure self-motivated intelligence. This *Nous* dwells in all things and is the soul of the world. And so we have come to the atomic systems of Anaxagoras and his successor, Democritus (born *c.* 460 B.C.). Democritus denied any controlling *Nous* and, following Pythagoras, said that everything depended on number and arrangement. To him the 'soul of the world' was Fire, and this fire was made up of all the atoms, all mixed up with nothing, with the whole in continual motion.

We have sketched this general development in order to give some sort of picture of the heritage into which the great philosophers of Greece entered. Socrates is said to have referred to an intelligence in everything, and to a divine purpose which has to do with the guidance of man, though the tendency to use the neuter rather than the masculine renders it uncertain to what extent he thought of this intelligence as personal. But to Plato there is an all-pervading intelligence (*Nous*), and he also speaks of the divine reason (*logos*) and of the divine knowledge (*episteme*) and of wisdom (*sophia*). He believes that there is a divine soul which is everywhere present.

But Plato has to deal with the hiatus between the supreme and perfect Creator and the imperfect creation. He followed Socrates in maintaining that there is a fixity in the universe, but it is to be found in thought. The essential characteristic of a thing remains the same whatever changes time may bring in its form. This essential characteristic is the idea, and it belongs to the realm of ideas. This realm is fixed, immutable, and has true and abiding existence. Plato thus pointed to what was true in the scheme of Parmenides, who denied there was any change; and at the same time he pointed to what was true in the scheme of Herakleitos, who denied that there was any fixity in things. Parmenides was talking about the realm of ideas. Herakleitos was talking about this phenomenal world. So far so good, but Plato was now faced with a yawning gap between the two. He attempted to fill this gap with the notion of 'the soul of the universe (*Ho kosmos*)', but he himself seems always to have been conscious of this difficulty.

In Aristotle we get the problem of the hiatus made stark and clear. There is the Prime Mover, the Absolute (*Ho On*), transcendent and alone, impassive, unchangeable, wholly outside all change and all the range of human striving. He is entirely apart from His creation, and from Him man receives neither help nor sympathy.

The Stoics sought to bridge the gap, and they did it by reviving the ancient *logos* suggestion of Herakleitos, allying with it the divine purpose of Socrates. The logos is divine, the eternal reason, unfolding itself most of all in beauty and order. It extends throughout all the universe (*kosmos*). By it all things exist and cohere. It carries in itself that seed-life which develops to its destined end. Hence it is called the *logos spermatikos* (the seed-logos). It acts as a general providence. It inspires all virtuous actions and guides the whole universe for good. It binds all things together into one coherent and harmonious whole. Man must live according to this righteous, upright logos (*orthos logos*); that is, to use the great Stoic phrase 'he must live according to nature' (i.e. according to the inner nature of things), and then all will be well. He will be at peace with all created things and at peace within himself. And this latter, said the Stoics, is necessarily so, because man himself is part of this whole. There is in man a finer essence of this *logos spermatikos*, and it is this 'common (*koinē*) *logos*' which constitutes human nature, and makes it what it is. This *logos* indwelling in man is to be discerned in two aspects. First there is the *logos endiathetos* (the indwelling reason), and secondly there is the *logos prophorikos* (the expressed thought).

This *logos*-doctrine of the Stoics became the popular doctrine of the Mediterranean world during the first century B.C., and the Jews of the Dispersion became especially subject to its influence. This is noticeable particularly in the writings which emanate from Alexandria. The deliberate attempt to harmonise Hebrew and Greek thought is the work of Philo, a Jew of Alexandria, born *c*. 20–10 B.C. Philo combined an unswerving allegiance to the Law of Moses with a passionate devotion to the philosophy of the Greeks. His eclectic system is the result.

The key to Philo's doctrine of the logos is to be found in the double aspect of the Stoic doctrine of the *logos spermatikos* as it is found in man, i.e. the *logos endiathetos* as the indwelling reason, and the *logos prophorikos* as the expressed word. This distinction is found in Aristotle with his '*logos* in the soul' and his 'external *logos*', and it corresponds roughly to what we should call the subjective and objective elements in human experience, particularly in respect of thought as being subjective, and expression or action as being objective. And so in Philo the same two elements appear, the logos as the Thought of God dwelling subjectively in the divine mind, and the logos as the expression of the Thought of God uttered and expressed in the created universe.

Now here there is a difference between Philo and the Stoics, and the difference is fundamental, for Philo began as a Jew and finished as a Jew, in spite of all his eclecticism and philosophising. Philo's logos is in part, but only in part, the *logos spermatikos* of the Stoics. The two are identical in so far as both are thought of as the eternal reason unfolding itself-himself in beauty and order and so forth. The difference comes in because the Stoic did not think of 'God' as being anything other that this distributed *logos*. Philo did think of God as in a very real sense separate from it. Philo added the idea of Aristotle's Prime Mover (First Cause) to the Stoic *logos spermatikos*, but being a good Jew he thought of the Prime Mover as a person, and in this respect moved directly away from Aristotle, since it is very doubtful whether Aristotle ever approached any idea of personality in his Absolute. He certainly divested his idea of any notion of change. The result of this equation of Philo's was to endow the Prime Mover, He now being most emphatically a person, with the divine equivalent of what, for the Stoics, in man was the *logos endiathetos* (indwelling *logos*, reason) and the *logos prophorikos* (uttered *logos*, word, expression). We thus arrive at the following: the logos as the Thought of God dwelling subjectively in the infinite mind and corresponding to the *logos endiathetos* in man; the logos as the expression of the Thought of God expressed objectively in the created Kosmos and corresponding to the *logos*

prophorikos in man. Philo nowhere uses this analogy.
Indeed he seems deliberately to avoid it, an understandable
action for a good Jew, who knew from as far back as
Hosea (*9*. 9) that God definitely was not man.

This problem of bridging the hiatus between God and
man, ideas and phenomena, is the greatest problem of all.
It appears in the Platonic system in the hiatus between the
world of ideas and the phenomenal world, that is the
world where things actually happen. It is said that in his
later works Plato did his best to bridge this gap of which
he was aware at least as clearly as any of his contemporaries,
perhaps as aware of it as the majority of his successors.
With Plato the hiatus is, so to speak, at the bottom end,
i.e., not between the ideas and the idea of ideas (his
'God'), but at the lower end, between the world of ideas
and this visible 'sensible' (i.e. of the senses), which always
seems to be most real to us in spite of the obvious fact that
it is always changing and becoming different. With
Aristotle the hiatus was more at the top end, and was involved in his separation of the Prime Mover from the
created world and from even Plato's world of ideas. The
Stoics avoided the gap by having a creation without any
creator, much as many moderns do. Philo attempts to
be more thorough with his eclectic system, but he ends by
having two hiatuses. He never really gets rid of Aristotle's
hiatus, and he never really bridges Plato's hiatus. Philo
has three categories. First, Aristotle's Absolute, who is
nevertheless a person. Secondly, the logos plus the
'powers' and the world of thought (*kosmos noetos*). Thirdly,
the world of the senses (*kosmos aisthetos*). Philo's 'powers'
(*dunameis*) correspond to Plato's ideas, and like them they
are 'immaterial' (*asomatoi*). They are intended to be the
connecting link between the Creator and the created,
between the Cause and that which is caused. They are
the connecting links of the Kosmos, that is, of the ordered
world which was created out of inert matter. But since,

with Philo equally as with Plato, they are incorporeal (immaterial), there is still no true link between the two worlds, the ideal and the phenomenal, the world of thought and the world of action. The hiatus therefore remains. At the same time Philo has kept closely enough to Aristotle to put the Prime Mover in a category, so to speak, by Himself, attracted doubtless to this by his fervent Judaism which held him, in spite of all his desire for an all-inclusive harmony, to the transcendence of God. Probably, even apart from Aristotle, Philo would have thought of God as in a separate category from all else. His debt to Aristotle was that he found himself doing this both as a good Jew and as a faithful philosopher.

In the *Gospel According to St. John* we find the solution, for there can be no means of bridging the gap which philosophy leaves except by 'telescoping' one category into another. Christianity achieves a harmony in the Incarnation, whereby the logos not only was with God, but was God, and also 'became flesh', that is, also broke into Philo's third category, and appeared in this *kosmos aisthetos* (world of the senses) of which we are 'sensibly' aware. Philo himself goes so far as to call the logos 'the second God'. Whatever exactly this meant to a good Jew, it is an evident attempt to telescope the first category (The Absolute) into the second. The Christian revelation is that God Himself without intermediary has Himself appeared in all three categories, and He Himself is the link.

The fact that the figure of wisdom is also in some sense an attempt to forge a connection between the transcendent God and the phenomenal world involves a consideration as to the relation of wisdom to the logos. This approximation is found, apart from Philo, most closely in *The Wisdom of Solomon*. Normally, the practical emphasis of wisdom (*chokmah*) led to an approximation rather with the Law.

We have already seen, both in Prov. *8*. 22f, and in
Ecclus. *1*. 4, 9; *24*. 9, that wisdom had come to be regarded
as in some sense God's instrument in Creation. The
identification of wisdom with the logos is carried further
in *The Wisdom of Solomon*. For instance, in 7. 22, we read
'Wisdom, which is the worker of all things, taught me'.
Or again (*18*. 15), 'Thine almighty word (*logos*) leaped
down from heaven out of Thy royal Throne, as a fierce
man of war . . . and brought Thine unfeigned commandment.' Yet again, we get the parallelism complete in
9. 1, 2 : 'O God of my fathers, who hast made all things
with Thy word (*logos*), and ordained man through Thy
wisdom (*sophia*)'. We get the full description of wisdom
in 7. 22ff, a passage which is full of words which are applied
to the logos, both amongst the Stoics and in Philo.
'There is in her a spirit intelligent (*pneuma noeron*), holy,
only-begotten (*monogenes*), manifold (*polumeres*), rarefied
(so Anaxagoras of his cosmic *nous*, intelligence), mobile,
piercing, undefiled, clear (i.e. pure like light and clear in
utterance), incapable of harm (either passively or actively),
loving the good, keen, unimpeded, beneficent, loving
toward men (philanthropic), unchangeable, reliable in its
working, all-powerful, all-surveying, and penetrating
through all spirits that are intelligent, pure, and most
rarefied. For wisdom is more mobile than any motion :
yea, she pervadeth and penetrateth all things by reason
of her pureness', and so the passage continues, showing
evident knowledge of the philosophers of Alexandria.

We are close to the position of Philo to whom, for the
most part, wisdom and logos are largely convertible
terms.* But we must always beware of ascribing to Greek
influence more than is right. Amongst the Jews of Palestine, who, so far as the orthodox were concerned, were not
influenced to nearly the same extent by Hellenistic ideas

* For a full discussion of this relationship, see DRUMMOND: *Philo
Judæus* (London, 1888), Vol. II, pp. 201–13.

M

as their brethren of the Dispersion, there was a tendency to personify the Word of God. The tendency arose out of the same need to bridge the gulf between the transcendent God and this changing world which He created. The fullest use was therefore made of the account of Creation which is found in the first chapter of *Genesis*, particularly of such passages as: 'And God said, Let there be light, and light came to be'. To a lesser degree, similar support was found in Psalm *29*, with its sevenfold glorification of 'the Voice of the Lord' as being effective in this created world. Accordingly we find a development of the use of the Aramaic *Memra* (strictly *Mē-mĕ-ra*, with the second '*e*' very short indeed) to denote the self-manifestation of God. Many writers have found in this usage the meaning of the use of the word logos in the prologue of the *Gospel According to St. John*. In our view this is unlikely, since the word *Memra* is not found by itself, but always in the forms 'The Memra of the Lord', or 'His (My, Thy, etc.) Memra'. It is well-nigh impossible that any Jew should use the word Memra by itself in the way in which the Greek word, *logos*, could be used. The development of the use of this word is nevertheless an indication of the need felt in Palestine, equally as amongst the Jews of the Dispersion, for some medium of manifestation in this world of the Only and Holy God. Accordingly such a word as 'His-Memra' is found regularly in the Targums as a paraphrase for the Holy Name itself, to avoid the slightest suggestion of an anthropomorphism. For instance, the Targum of Onkelos in Gen. *3*. 8 has: 'And they heard the voice of the Word of the Lord God walking in the garden . . .'

CHAPTER XVII

TEMPLE AND SYNAGOGUE

THE rebuilding of the Temple was begun in the year 520 B.C., and carried through by Zerubbabel and Jeshua under the encouragement of the prophet Haggai. It was from the beginning a rallying point for the separatists. The people round about, those who had never been out of Palestine, were willing and eager to help in the work of restoration, but they were rebuffed with the words: 'Ye have nothing to do with us to build an house unto our God' (Ezra 4. 3). From that time the builders met with every kind of hindrance on the part of 'the people of the land', but the rebuilding was completed, according to Ezra 2. 15, on the third day of the month Adar, in the sixth year of Darius I (Hystaspis), that is, in March, 516 B.C., though Josephus says (*Ant. Iud.* XI, IV, 7) that it took them seven years. We know very little of the details of the building, except that it was not to be compared for splendour with the Temple which Solomon had built; so Hag. 2. 3, and perhaps Zech. 4. 10. This comparison is amplified by Josephus, who says (*Ant. Iud.* XI, IV, 2) that it was the priests and the Levites and the elder part of the families who were distressed, but that the people in general were glad to get any sort of a Temple built on any terms. He says also (*ibid.*, XI, IV, 7) that 'the Jews also built the cloisters of the inner Temple that were round about the Temple itself', and he refers to the various gates at which the proper allocations of porters were stationed.

It is evident that considerable additions were made to the Temple buildings during the centuries that followed.

According to Ben-Sira (Ecclus. *50*. 1–3), the Temple was renovated in the time of Simeon ben-Jochanan, who also fortified it, and dug out a huge reservoir. This High Priest Simeon was probably Simeon II, the son of Jochanan II, a contemporary of Ben-Sira himself, who lived in the times of Antiochus III (the Great, 223–187 B.C.). Some scholars think that the builder was Simeon I, the son of Jochanan I, who lived about a hundred years earlier. There is some confirmation of the later date in Josephus (*Ant. Iud.* XII, III, 3), where it is stated that after his victory over Ptolemy V (Epiphanes, 203–181/0 B.C.) in 199 B.C., Antiochus the Great desired that the work about the Temple should be finished, 'and the cloisters, and if there is anything else that ought to be rebuilt'.

The Temple buildings were probably damaged more than once, and perhaps seriously, before this restoration at the beginning of the second century B.C. They may have suffered during the suppression by Artaxerxes III (Ochus) of the rebellion of 351 B.C., and again when Jerusalem was seriously damaged by Ptolemy I (Soter) in 312 B.C. It was in the time of Antiochus IV (Epiphanes, 175–163 B.C.) that the Temple probably suffered most. According to Polybius (XXXI, 4), this king plundered most of the temples on which he could lay his hands, so that the Temple at Jerusalem suffered with the rest, apart from the troubles of the Maccabæan Revolt. In those days, the king robbed the Temple of all its treasures, and took away the golden candlesticks, the golden altar of incense and table for the shewbread, and even the veils of fine linen and scarlet.* According to 1 Macc. *4*. 38, the sanctuary was laid desolate, the gates burned up, the priests' chambers pulled down, and there were 'shrubs growing in courts as in a forest or as on one of the mountains'. After three and a half years the worship was restored, but troubles were by no means at an end. In the days of Judas, the

* Josephus: *Ant. Iud.*, XII, v. 4.

Temple had two courts, into the inner of which only the priests and the Israelites could enter. After the death of Judas, Alkimus the High Priest, the nominee of the Seleucids appointed by Lysias and reinstated by Bacchides, began to pull down the inner wall, so as to make one court only, to which Gentiles as well as Jews should have access. But he was seized with a palsy before the work had proceeded very far (1 Macc. 9. 54–56). Josephus (*Ant. Iud.* XII, x, 6) says that this took place before the death of Judas, and that subsequently 'the people bestowed the High-priesthood on Judas', but this is unlikely. In after years fortifications were added to the Temple buildings, by Jonathan, the brother of Judas Maccabæus, and especially by John Hyrcanus (134/133—104/103 B.C.), the first of the Hasmonæan priest-kings. It is probable that he also built the great bridge which spanned the Tyropœan Valley at the south-west corner of the Temple Mount.

The major change within the Temple precincts proper is dated from the time of Alexander Jannæus (102/101—76/75 B.C.), who was pelted with citrons by the people because of his deliberate slackness in the matter of the ritual of the Feast of Tabernacles. Josephus says (*Ant. Iud.* XIII, XIII, 5) that he built a wooden partition wall round the Altar and the Temple and 'by this he obstructed the multitude from coming at him'. It extended 'as far as that partition within which it was lawful only for the priests to enter', so that here we have the beginning of the Court of the Priests as distinct from the Court of Israel.

When Pompey breached the Temple walls after a three months' siege the priests were cut down as they calmly continued their Sabbath sacrifices, but Pompey, though he marched into the empty Holy of Holies, touched nothing of the furnishings or the Temple treasure 'on account of his regard for religion, and in this point also he acted in a manner that was worthy of his virtue'. This is the statement of Josephus (*Ant. Iud.* XIV, IV, 4), and it is confirmed by Cicero (*Pro Flacco*, 67), who said that he 'did not touch anything belonging to that temple'. Crassus was not so forbearing, for he plundered the Temple ruthlessly in 54 B.C., and the buildings suffered considerably when Herod the Great stormed the city and Temple in 37 B.C. with the help of Antony's general, Sosius. Parts of the cloisters were then reduced to ashes, but Herod was a great builder and in his days the Temple buildings rose in such magnificence as had never before been seen.

Herod the Great began rebuilding the Temple and extending it in the year 20–19 B.C. The sanctuary was completed in eighteen months by a thousand energetic priests, but the rest was still being rebuilt in the time of Jesus (Mark *13*. 1. John *2*. 20). The walls were built in white marble, and the whole edifice looked like a mountain covered with snow. All the eastern front was plated with gold. Terraces rose one above the other, and the courts were surrounded by colonnades and pierced with gates overlaid with gold.

According to Josephus (*Contra Apionem*, I, 22) the size of the Temple area in the third century B.C. was about 500 feet by about 150 feet. This may refer to the buildings proper and not to the whole area which subsequently was known as the Court of the Gentiles. Herod certainly extended this area, and in his time it had an area of 400 yards by 330 yards. The Temple buildings were normally reached by the bridge over the Tyropœan Valley, 354 feet long and 50 feet wide, with a drop of over 200 feet into the valley below. The bridge and roadway led straight into the Royal Porch which extended along the south side of the Court of the Gentiles, the large level enclosure towards the north end of which the Temple buildings proper stood. This Royal Porch contained two double rows of columns, with a central avenue 45 feet wide, the height of these cloisters being 100 feet. There were cloisters on all four sides, those on the other three sides being composed of three rows of columns. At the eastern side the columns were known as Solomon's Porch, and it was here that Jesus talked (John *10*. 23) and Peter preached (Acts *3*. 1ff). These columns were supposed to be a survival from the original Temple which Solomon built.

The Temple itself stood in the northern half of the Court of the Gentiles, and to the west rather than to the east. Worshippers usually entered the Temple precincts over the Tyropœan Bridge, crossed the Court of the Gentiles diagonally to the left, and then made almost a full left turn to enter by the eastern Gate of the Temple, known as the Beautiful Gate. The whole structure was enclosed by a screen of marble, $4\frac{1}{2}$ feet in height, and beyond this no Gentile must pass. This marble screen had warnings cut into it, and part of such an inscription has been found. It is written in Greek capital letters, and says: 'No foreigner may enter within the screen and enclosure round the Holy Place. Whosoever is caught so trespassing, will himself be the cause of death overtaking him'. Inside the screen there were fourteen steps on all sides except the west, where the Holy of Holies stood, there being no way up on that side. At the top of the fourteen steps there was a wall 40 feet high, a fortification (*chel*). Here in the last stages of the Jewish War (66–70 A.D.), the defenders held the Romans at bay even after the cloisters had been burnt and destroyed.

The Beautiful Gate of the Temple was the only gate which pierced the fortification on the eastern side, but on the north and the south there were four gates each. The Beautiful Gate led into the Court of the Women, and it was here that the worshippers stood whilst the Temple ritual was being observed, prostrating themselves at intervals according to custom. Near the entrance to this court there were thirteen chests, and into these chests, called 'trumpets' because of their shape, the worshippers cast their gifts, choosing their 'trumpet' according to the use to which they desired their gifts to be put. Tradition has it that the women were allowed to enter the sacred precincts as far as this court, and that they occupied the galleries which surrounded it on three sides, east, north and south.

From the Court of the Gentiles there was a flight of fifteen semi-circular steps, which led through the Gate of Nicanor into the Court of Israel. This gate was built in commemoration of the victory over Nicanor, whom Judas Maccabæus defeated and slew at the battle of Adasa in the pass of Beth-horon early in the year 160 B.C. If any man suspected his wife of infidelity, he brought her to the Temple before the priest for the ordeal of jealousy, and it was in this gate that they both stood. The gate was of wrought Corinthian bronze, and it was 75 feet high and nearly as broad. It is probable that at one time there was no Court of the Women, and then this Gate of Nicanor would be the outer gate of the Temple, as some ancient traditions speak of it.

There is much uncertainty as to the exact dimensions of the Court of Israel, but beyond it and separated by a low wall there was the Court of the Priests, into which none but the priests might enter. Directly in line from the Gate of Nicanor and the other side of the low wall, there stood the Altar of Burnt Offering, a massive structure of unhewn stones, fastened together with mortar, pitch and molten lead. The base of the altar was 32 cubits square by 1 cubit deep, the cubit being just short of 20 inches. Based on this, the structure itself was 5 cubits high, and was 30 cubits square, so that there was a ledge all round of 1 cubit's width. The horns of the altar jutted out at this level, and above it there was the hearth itself, 24 cubits square, with a ledge all round of 1 cubit's width for the priests to stand on at a convenient level below the flat surface on top where the sacrifice was burned. There was a ramp of masonry which led up to this ledge on which the priests stood, and at one period there was a foot-race up this ramp on the Day of Atonement, until one year a priest was seriously injured, when the custom was abandoned.

Beyond the altar there rose the massive porch which stood before the Sanctuary itself. This porch was 172 feet high and as broad, though the Holy Place behind it was but 120 feet broad. There were double golden doors below covered with a veil of finest Babylonian material, embroidered in purple and in blue. Above, there was a magnificent golden vine, with huge clusters some 6 feet long and with large branches hanging down from a great height. Inside the Sanctuary there were the seven-branched candlestick, the altar of incense and the table for the shew-bread. Beyond this was the Holy of Holies itself, empty of all furniture. Here was the Presence of the Lord God Himself, and none entered except the High Priest, once a year on the Day of Atonement, and then he pronounced the Sacred Name.

The Temple personnel varied in its constitution through the centuries. The original Jerusalem priesthood was Zadokite, and it is probable that Zadok was priest before David captured the citadel in the eighth year of his reign. Abiathar, the sole survivor of the massacre by Saul of the ancient House of Eli, priests of the Ark from Egypt (1 Sam. 2. 27f), had shared with David all his early vicissitudes, and he shared the Jerusalem priesthood with Zadok in the days of David's prosperity. When the throne was seized on behalf of Solomon, Abiathar found himself on the losing side, and was the sole survivor of Adonijah's supporters, owing his life, beyond doubt, to the fact that he was a priest of God. For ever afterwards the Zadokites were priests of the Temple of Jerusalem. Josiah made an attempt to provide a place there for the Levitical priests of the south whose shrines he destroyed, but the Zadokite priests resisted this (2 Kings 23. 9). After the Exile, we find the Jerusalem priests styled 'the priests, the sons of Aaron', but sixteen of the twenty-four courses into which they were divided were Zadokites. These were the sacrificing priests during the major part, indeed all the later period, of the Second Temple. The Levites became ministering officials of one type and another, and it was not until the last days of the Temple, in the time of Herod Agrippa II, that they were allowed to wear the white robes of the priesthood. The Asaphites were choristers in the Temple choirs. The Qorachites (Korahites) became door-keepers in these post-exilic days, though there is evidence that at one time they held a much more exalted rank.

In earlier post-exilic days the musical instruments used in the Temple services consisted of trumpets, psalteries and harps, timbrels, stringed instruments and pipes, and two types of cymbals (Ps. *150*), but in Herod's time these were supplemented by an organ (*magrephah*) which had thirteen pipes and two bellows. Tradition says that it could be made to sound a hundred different notes. In those days the normal orchestra consisted of six lutes, six harps, two pairs of cymbals, two trumpets, and between two and twelve flutes. There is an ancient tradition that in earlier days there were women singers in the Temple choirs, but in later times the soprano parts were provided by boys.

Post-exilic times saw a steady development in the ritual, and it is possible that most of these changes were due to Babylonian influences. Certainly the use of sweet spices for incense was a post-exilic introduction; indeed there does not seem to have been any incense used at all in pre-exilic times. After the Exile the gift-offering (*minchah*) came to be always the cereal-offering which accompanied the meat-offering (*zebach*), and it was followed by an appropriate drink-offering. There was developed also a whole system of sin-offerings (*chattath*) and guilt-offerings ('*asham*), both of them having to do with ritual offences and compensation payments.

The central feature of the normal Temple worship was the sacrifices, morning and evening, i.e. at dawn and at the ninth hour (3 p.m.). Whilst the burnt offerings were being consumed, the priests blew with their trumpets and the cymbals clashed. Then the drink-offerings of water and wine were poured out, and the daily psalm was sung. This was in accordance with the ancient adage, 'There is no song except over wine'. According to the Mishnah tradition, the psalm varied according to the day of the week, Ps. *24* for the first day, and then Pss. *48, 82, 94, 81, 93*, and, for the Sabbath, *92*. Each psalm was sung in three stanzas, with an interval between, in which the priests blew with their trumpets and the people prostrated themselves. The theory was that all Israel had to be present at these daily sacrifices. Palestine therefore was divided up into twenty-four sections, corresponding to the twenty-four courses of the priesthood, and each section represented all Israel in its turn. Since it was obviously impossible for all the men in any one section to be present at one and the same time, a deputation was sent to represent the whole section at the sacrifices, whilst the pious gathered at home in their local synagogue for prayer at the time when the sacrifices were being offered up. Each course of priests was changed on the Sabbath, the incoming priests taking charge of the evening sacrifice and changing the shew-bread.

On the Sabbath there were additional sacrifices, and a Sabbath canticle was sung. The morning canticle was the Deuteronomic Song of Moses (Deut. *32*), and it was sung in six portions on six successive Sabbaths. The afternoon canticle was the Exodus Song of Moses (Exod. *15*) and the Song of Israel (Num. *21*. 17f), making three sections in all, the Exodus canticle being divided into two portions. These were certainly part of the ritual before the Christian era, though how long they had been so used is not known. There is evidence that Ps. *105*. 1–15 and

Ps. *96* at one time played a conspicuous part in the service, since the Chronicler evidently knew exactly what he was about in his description of the Temple service of his own day (1 Chron. *16*), for it is generally recognised that it was his custom to dress former times in the garments of his own time. He evidently is following a well-known custom when he adds the couplet: 'O give thanks unto the Lord . . .' to the psalms which the Asaphite choirs sang (1 Chron. *16*. 34), and he knew the nature of the rubrics at the end of Ps. *106*, 47f (cf. 1 Chron. *16*. 35f).

There were also special psalms for the festivals and feasts; *135* for Passover, *81* for New Moons, and *30* for the Feast of Dedication. The Hallel ('praise'), namely Pss. *113–118*, was sung at the three great pilgrimage feasts, with varying accompaniments, movements and responses, all varying according to the particular feast. At the Feast of Passover, for instance, the response of the people involved the repetition of the first verse of each of the six psalms, and they interjected 'Hallelujah' ('Praise ye the Lord') at the end of every other line. But when they came to the last of the six psalms they repeated 'Hallelujah' thrice, and also the three lines which comprise verses 25 and 26. At Tabernacles, the priests marched in procession round the altar whilst verse 25 in Ps. 118 was being sung. The orchestral accompaniment varied from feast to feast. At Tabernacles, flutes were used, but not on the first day or on the Sabbath. There was no accompaniment at Passover, and one flute only at Pentecost (Weeks). There is a general description of the Sabbath service in all its splendour during the second century B.C., in Ecclus. *50*. 5–21, where Ben-Sira has described what he himself had seen with his own eyes.

There were also many other customs and rites performed apart from the sacrifices, whether the regular daily sacrifices or sin-offerings or freewill offerings of whatever type. The most splendid of all the rites was the great all-night festival

of the Feast of Tabernacles. This was the great Harvest
Festival at the end of the agricultural year, and during the
opening ceremonies there were two particular celebrations
which must go back into far antiquity. The opening
night of the Feast of Tabernacles coincided with the night
of the Harvest full moon. This particular night was the
occasion of an all-night festival, when the Court of the
Women was lit up by giant candelabras. So bright was
the light from these four great lamps that it is said every
court in Jerusalem was lit up. The common people were
accommodated in galleries round the court and, down
below, young priests danced with lighted torches, tossing
them high and catching them, and all the while whirling
in acrobatic dances. Meanwhile the Levitical choirs
stood on the fifteen steps which led up to the Gate of
Nicanor, and played and sang the whole night through.
It is said that they sang the fifteen Songs of Degrees (step-
songs), Pss. *120–134*, though some deny this. Just before
the dawn two priests appeared in the Gate of Nicanor, and
blew thrice with their trumpets. When they reached the
tenth step they stood still and blew another blast, and yet
another when they reached the level of the court below.
They then marched straight through the court to the
Beautiful Gate of the Temple, timing their arrival there to
coincide with the first rays of the sun as it appeared over
the ridge of the Mount of Olives. They then turned
their backs to the sun and chanted, as they faced the Holy
of Holies, 'Our fathers who were in this place turned their
backs to the Temple and their faces to the east, and
prostrated themselves to the rising sun; but we lift our
eyes to God'.

The appearance of the sun over the summit of the Mount
of Olives was the signal for the offering of the morning
sacrifice. When the time for the following drink-offering
came on this particular occasion, a priest was there ready
beside the two funnels which were close beside the Altar

of Burnt Offering. He had been down to the Pool of Siloam to draw water specially with a golden pitcher. Normally the water for the drink-offering was brought in overnight, but not on this occasion. This was the time for 'drawing water with joy out of the wells of salvation', as Isa. *12.* 3 puts it. It is doubtless the case that the records of many ancient rites and customs of the Temple ritual have long since been lost, though these and others are preserved in various Jewish writings, the Mishnah, and the various Toseftas and the Talmuds.

The other great institution in the life of post-exilic Jewry was the synagogue, independent of the Temple, but complementary rather than antagonistic. The origin of the synagogue is a matter of dispute. Some maintain that its origin is to be found in the circumstances of the Babylonian Exile, when the Jews may be presumed to have gathered together to strengthen themselves and each other in their devotion to the religion of their fathers. Jewish tradition is strong that the synagogue is as old as Ezra, which may mean nothing more than that it was recognised by Jews of the first century of our era as being an ancient and well-established institution. Some scholars of the present day deny that there were any synagogues in Palestine before the time of the Maccabees. In any case, it is true that there were synagogues outside Palestine before there were synagogues inside Palestine, whether in Babylon during the Babylonian Exile or in the Dispersion generally.

Synagogues were more than barely religious institutions, and amongst the Dispersion generally they acted as the civic centre also for the community, and especially as schools. The whole atmosphere tends to some extent to be more secular than that of a normal Christian place of meeting, and there is much more noise and moving about. Originally there were religious services in the synagogues on three days in the week, on the Sabbath, and on Monday and on Thursday, but later there were three services a day, at the third hour (9 a.m.), the sixth hour (noon), and the ninth hour (3 p.m.).

The earliest element of the synagogue service was the Reading of the Law, which was in Hebrew, followed by an explanation in the vernacular Aramaic. The natural development from this was a discourse, since the original function of the synagogue seems to have been that of teaching. Possibly the Reading from the Law was preceded by prayer, and in the prayers was embodied at an early date the *Shema'*. This consisted of three passages from the Law, Deut. *6*. 4–9; *11*. 13–21. Num. *15*. 37–41; and it was so called because of its opening word, which means 'Hear'.

The earliest Readings from the Law seems to have been introduced as early as *c*. 300 B.C. in connection with certain festivals. At first the passages which were read were from Lev. *23*, and they consisted of the passages relevant to the particular festival. In course of time these readings were extended to the four special Sabbaths in the month Adar, the last month of the civil year, and finally to every Sabbath. Finally, in Palestine, the whole of the Law was arranged in portions to be read Sabbath by Sabbath over a period of three years. The modern custom is to read through the Law once every year, and this was the way in which the Law was read amongst the Babylonian Jews.

There came a time, probably owing to disputes with the Samaritans as to the proper way of observing festivals, when the Law was 'concluded' with a verse or two from the Prophets. This Reading from the Prophets was called the *Haftarah* ('Conclusion'), and in time these developed also so that every portion of the Law (*Seder*) had its *Haftarah*. It is not known at what period this full development was in being, but it was probably about the beginning of this era and certainly well before the end of the first century A.D.

It has sometimes been conjectured that the Psalter was read through Sabbath by Sabbath over a three-year period, but there is no certain evidence of this. If this is the case, it is probable that the Readings from the Prophets were developed rather earlier.

Another development in the synagogical service is the prayer known as the Eighteen Benedictions (*Shemoneh Esreh*). These are still in use in the modern synagogue, though there are nineteen now, and they are sometimes called *Tefillah* (Prayer), and *Amidah* (Standing) because they are recited with everyone standing. Originally the Amidah consisted of six benedictions only, Nos. 1, 2, 3 and 17, 18, 19. They are known as *Aboth* (Fathers), *Geburoth* (Mighty Acts), *Qedushath hash-Shem* (Sanctification of the Name); and, for the concluding three, *Abodah* (Service), *Hoda'ah* (Thanksgiving), and *Birkath hakKohanim* (Blessing of the Priests). These two groups of three are said daily throughout the year, and this custom has been followed since very early times. The other intermediary Benedictions are recited on ordinary weekdays, but on Sabbaths and Festivals they give place to special prayers. Of the intermediary Benedictions, it is generally agreed that No. 12 was added about 100 A.D., whilst No. 15 (the one which brought the number up to nineteen) is probably as late as *c*. 250 A.D. Of the others, Nos. 10, 11, 13 and 15 are probably Maccabæan, and the remainder are earlier, except perhaps the seventh.

Another development associated with the synagogue is the growth of the Targums. These are Aramaic paraphrases of the original Hebrew Text. In the earlier times, say at the beginning of the Christian Era, the interpreter had an unenviable task. He was not supposed to have any Aramaic rendering written from which he could read. He had to translate three verses at a time. He must not translate word for word, but he must give the sense of the Hebrew. The custom goes back to Ezra, when he caused the Law to be read before all the people (Neh. *8*), and fourteen men, who are mentioned by name (verse 7), together with the Levites, explained what was read, making sure that the people understood it. By the second century A.D. there were written Targums, and the interpreter (*Meturgeman*) found his task somewhat simpler.

The most famous synagogue was in Alexandria, though Philo said that there were many synagogues in the various quarters of the city. It is said, for instance, that at the time when the Temple was destroyed by the Romans under Titus there were 394 synagogues in Jerusalem, though another tradition avers that there were 480. The two most ancient synagogues in Babylonia were that of Nahardea, which tradition says was founded by King Jehoiachin himself, and that of Huzal. As early as the time of Augustus Cæsar there were many synagogues in Rome. Indeed, by the time of the first century A.D. the Jews were scattered far and wide, and there was a synagogue wherever the necessary quorum of ten males could be obtained. Later the custom developed of there being ten 'men of leisure' maintained by the wealthier communities so that the daily service could always be held.

In the Greek synagogues, for instance, the synagogues of Alexandria, it was the custom to read the scriptures in the Greek translation (*Septuagint*). There is an ancient tradition, embodied in a pseudograph called *The Letter of Aristeas* (possibly in its present form as late as the beginning of the Christian Era, though opinion varies considerably), that the Hebrew Old Testament was translated in the time of Ptolemy II (Philadelphos, 285–246 B.C.). He was urged by his librarian, Demetrius Phalcreus, to send to the High Priest, Eleazar, for seventy (or seventy-two) scholars who should perform this task. Hence the same *Septuagint* (seventy). Tradition varies as to the actual year of his reign in which this was supposed to have taken place, the various figures being given as the 2nd, the 17th, the 19th,

and the 20th. The day is generally agreed, in the traditions, to be the 8th of the month Tebet (towards the end
of December or the beginning of January), coinciding
with a naval victory in the war against Antigonus. Later
Jews, when the Christians had adopted the Septuagint
Version in their contentions with the Jews, called this
particular day the fast of darkness, and regarded it as
comparable with the 'day on which the golden calf was
made'. Alexandrian Jews, however, and Jews of the
Dispersion generally, found the Greek Version of inestimable value.

Modern opinion regards the ancient tradition as en-
shrining the truth that a beginning of the translation was
made into Greek about the middle of the third century
B.C., the part translated being the Law itself, i.e. the five
Books of Moses. The rest was translated by various
scholars during the next two centuries or so. It is not
thought that the tradition is correct in stating that the
translation was for Ptolemy's library, but rather that the
Alexandrian Jews translated the books to meet their own
need. In any case this translation was of inestimable
value in spreading the knowledge of the Jewish faith
through the Græco-Roman world, and it formed the
Christian Bible during the first years of the Church.
Indeed, the Old Testament of the Christians was this Greek
translation until Jerome's Latin Bible, the Vulgate, was
adopted at the beginning of the fourth century A.D. It
has a great value for modern textual scholars in that there
are many instances in which it preserves a sounder text
than the orthodox Hebrew Version.

CHAPTER XVIII

PHARISEES, SADDUCEES AND ESSENES

EVERY reader of the New Testament is familiar with
groups of men, united by common beliefs and customs,
such as the Pharisees, the Sadducees, and, to a lesser degree,
the Essenes. All these sects were largely the product of
the period between the completion of the Old Testament
and the beginning of the Christian Era, though some of
their differences go back in their origins to the early post-
exilic period.

Josephus (*Ant. Iud.* XIII, v, 9) mentions these three sects
as existing in the time of Jonathan, High Priest from
160/159—142/141 B.C., the brother of Judas Maccabæus and
Judas's successor in the leadership of the Jews. Josephus
gives a short account of the beliefs of the three parties, and
refers the reader to his *Wars of the Jews* for fuller information, the details being found in *Bell. Iud.* II, VIII, 2–14.
In *Ant. Iud.* XIII, x, 5–6, Josephus gives an account of the
breach between John Hyrcanus (134/133—104/103 B.C.)
and the Pharisees. We have told this story on p. 46, where
it will be seen that already there was a considerable amount
of rivalry between the two parties, amounting to much
bitterness and even open quarrelling. It is evident that
at this time, whatever may have been the position before
and after, the rivalry was political at least as much as
religious. The Pharisees objected to the combination of
the high-priesthood and the civil authority, and held that
John Hyrcanus ought to content himself with the civil
power only. The fact that the complaint was brought up
under the guise of an insult against his mother shows that

there was a good deal of bad blood in the general attitude of the parties to each other.

Josephus has many references to the Pharisees, e.g. how they joined themselves to Alexandra Salome, 'to assist her in the government' after the death of her husband Alexander Jannæus in 76–75 B.C. (*Bell. Iud.* I, v, 2 ; *Ant. Iud.* XIII, xvi, 2). He says (*Ant. Iud.* XVII, ii, 4) that in the time of Herod the Great they 'were in a capacity of greatly opposing kings' and 'a cunning sect'. Their influence and authority during the reign of Alexandra Salome lasted nine years. Josephus has no great love for them, probably because of the part they played in opposition to Rome both before and during the Jewish War of 66–70 A.D. He says (*Bell. Iud.* I, v, 2) that they 'appear more religious than others, and seem to interpret the laws more accurately', and that they 'artfully insinuated themselves' into Salome's favour, so that they had all the power and she had all the expense of it. They became, said Josephus, very arrogant, and 'while she governed other people', 'the Pharisees governed her'.

There is considerable division of opinion concerning the origin of these two major parties, the Pharisees and the Sadducees, and the differences extend even to the origin and significance of their names.

An attempt has been made to trace the division and antagonism right back to the time when Solomon established Zadok as sole priest in Jerusalem to the exclusion of Abiathar,* but this suggestion can hardly be maintained. The weakness of the suggestion depends upon the reliance on the genealogies of the Priestly Code, which, like those in the writings of the Chronicler, can scarcely be as reliable as is maintained (see above, pp. 77f). It used to be held that the origin of the name 'Sadducees' is in the word

---

* See OESTERLEY: *The Jews and Judaism during the Greek Period* (London, 1941), pp. 240 f, who sets forth this point of view, following Aptowitzer.

tsaddiq (righteous), but this involves the letter '*i*' where there ought to be a '*u*', a change which cannot be justified. A. E. Cowley suggested that the name is Persian in origin and means 'infidel' (Persian *zindik*), and that it was given them because of their marked tendency to sympathise with Gentile ways and ideas. The suggestion which is now generally favoured, against the former opinion in favour of 'righteous ones', is that the name is connected with the name Zadok. Some suggest that this was an unknown Zadok who was outstanding in the party life at some unknown time, whilst others cling to the original Zadok of Solomon's time. This latter Zadok was of the original priesthood of Jerusalem, and the Zadokites never ceased to be priests there. Even after the Exile, when the priesthood was called 'Aaronic', there were still two-thirds of them who were Zadokites. We know that from the time of the Exile onwards the Jerusalem priests were by no means exclusive in their attitude. They favoured intermarriage with the heathen in Eliashib's time, and they were friendly with Sanballat, who apparently held some official office in Samaria under the Persians (Neh. *4*. 2). Their record in the days that preceded the Maccabæan revolt was far from satisfactory from the strictly Jewish point of view, and there is every indication that the priests were much more worldly than their office would warrant. The only difficulty in this last explanation is that of the 'double *d*', which cannot be explained on any orthodox lines, and seems to be due to some confusion with the word *tsaddiq* (righteous).

The name 'Pharisees' is an anglicised form of the Greek transcription of the Aramaic name *Perishaya*. Both this and the corresponding Hebrew form *Perushim* mean 'separated ones'. So much is certain. The difficulties lie in deciding how and why they received this name. One suggestion is that the Pharisees sought by the name to emphasise their separateness from the common people, but this suggestion

cannot be maintained, because the Pharisees were essentially the popular party, and had the support of the people.
This is the testimony of Josephus; from the time of John
Hyrcanus onwards, he says, 'while the Sadducees are able
to persuade none but the rich, and have not the populace
obsequious to them', yet 'the Pharisees have the multitude
on their side'. In a similar way, it is difficult to maintain
that they took this name themselves in order to emphasise
the difference between themselves and the Gentiles.
Certainly in the time of the Lord Jesus the Pharisees were
eager to make proselytes, and would 'compass sea and
land to make one' (Matt. 23. 15). The Mishnah, also,
for which they were largely responsible, is full of references
to dealings which Jews had with Gentiles, and it is unlikely that the Pharisees could have had any antagonism
to the Gentiles as such, exclusive though they were in some
respects.

The two suggestions which seem to be most probable
are the following. The first in concerned with their
anxiety for the proper and exact fulfilment of the Law, and
is the more likely. There is plenty of testimony to their
zeal in this particular, both in Josephus and in the Gospels.
They were separate in the sense that they 'made themselves
holy' by strict adherence to the Law. This was one of the
aims of orthodox Jewry, as we have seen (pp. 79). They
separated themselves from all those who were slack in these
matters. They were thus the core of all the faithfulness
to the Law which made Jewry a separate and a separated
people. In this respect they are the true successors of
those Chasidim whose fanaticism formed the wedge of
Judas Maccabæus's onslaught upon the Syrian Greeks.
Certainly what the Chasidim were in the fight against the
armies of Antiochus Epiphanes the Pharisees were in the
fight against the Romans in the last days of the Temple.

The second suggestion has to do with the activity of the
Pharisees in the synagogue, particularly in their function

of instructing the people. This task had once been the duty and the glory of the priesthood, but in post-exilic times the priests developed more and more into sacrificing officials. The Pharisees expounded Scripture in the synagogues. The Aramaic word from which 'Pharisee' comes is used to mean 'interpret' as well as 'separate', and many think that the word 'Pharisee' originally meant 'expounders', i.e. of the Law. The weakness of this suggestion is that the word is a passive form, whereas this suggestion would seem to demand an active form. We incline therefore to the first of these two latter suggestions, and hold that the word refers to the zeal with which the Pharisees kept the Law, and so were 'separated', 'made holy' (cf. the *hiphil*, or causative form of the verb *q-d-sh*, holy).

The origin of the Pharisees then is probably to be found in the *Chasidim*, those men who placed loyalty to the Law above everything else. The word *chasid* has a long history in Jewish religion, and is connected with the word *chesed* (usually translated 'mercy, loving-kindness)'. We have traced the development of this word elsewhere.* The word *chasid* came to mean those who were devoted to the Law. The word is found frequently in the Psalter, twenty-three times in all, and is translated variously 'holy ones, saints, pious ones'. In Ps. *149*. 1, 5, 9 it seems definitely to refer to the Chasidim of Maccabæan times, when they had become a definite party who stood for devoted piety to the Law in contrast to the worldly ways of the Hellenisers in Jewry. This is roughly the time when Josephus said that the two parties, Pharisees and Sadducees, came into existence. The attitude of the priests in these days suggests that the explanation (Zadok) of the name 'Sadducees' may not be very wide of the mark.

The Pharisees, as we have seen, were truly missionary in

---

* *The Distinctive Ideas of the Old Testament* (London, 1944), pp. 94–130.

their attitude to the Gentiles, but they were nevertheless strict in their observance of the Law. They preferred the old paths and were against all Gentile innovations. They took vows to observe in the strictest manner all the ordinances concerning Levitical purity, and to be extremely punctilious in the matter of paying tithes and all other dues enjoined in the Law. A full 'associate' (brother, Heb. *chaber*) was forbidden to buy from or sell to any 'sinner' (i.e. a man who did not keep the Law and was ritually 'unclean') anything that had to do with food and drink. He was forbidden to eat in the sinner's house, though he could entertain a 'sinner' as guest if he himself provided the clothes, since the sinner's own clothes might be ritually impure. All these rules give some substance to the interpretation of the name 'Pharisee' as one who separated himself from the common people, using this phrase to describe those who had neither the time nor the money (or perhaps the inclination) to observe all these details of the Levitical law as concerning ceremonial purity.

The scribes of the Pharisees were so insistent upon all these matters that they added rules of their own in order, as they said, 'to set a fence about the Law', lest even inadvertently they should transgress. Josephus tells us (*Ant. Iud.* XIII, x, 6) that the Pharisees 'have delivered to the people a great many observances from their fathers which are not written in the Law of Moses; and for that reason it is that the Sadducees reject them, and say that we are to esteem those observances to be obligatory which are in the written word, but are not to observe what are derived from the tradition of our forefathers.' The Pharisees, therefore, are the upholders of the Oral Tradition, as against the Sadducees.

The Sadducees held to the Law of Moses only, and did not accept either the Oral Tradition or even the Prophets as authoritative. They did not agree with the Pharisees, who believed in the resurrection of the body and future retribution, for they clung to the traditional Sheol doctrine. They were indifferent to all those Messianic anticipations which were strong amongst the Pharisees. They denied the existence of angels and spirits.

All these things which the Sadducees denied were dear to the Pharisees. These did indeed regard all things and all men as being dependent upon God, but they maintained that it was within man's power to do what was right. A man had two inclinations (*yetser*), a good *yetser* and a bad *yetser*, and it was for man, by faithfulness to the Law, to see to it that his good inclination triumphed. Man's works were in his own choice, and it was in a man's own power to do either right or wrong. A man's salvation, that is, is in his own hands, and he is saved by his works. It is easy to see how their particular beliefs easily earned for them the condemnation of the Lord Jesus. That there were faithful and devout Pharisees, no one would deny, and men such as Hillel were truly humble and religious in the best sense of the term. But the emphasis on Levitical purity tended to make the Law 'a manual of religious etiquette'. Their insistence on the exact observance of every detail tended to make them purely formal, and to lead them into an externalism which did not touch the real man beneath. Their belief in salvation by works engendered easily a pride and an ostentation and a self-righteousness which were one and all altogether undesirable. But in spite of all these inherent weaknesses in their system they were faithful to the Law, and in the dark days which preceded the destruction of the Temple their loyalty and devotion were beyond compare.

The Essenes arose during the second century B.C., and were a strict community from the beginning. There is some evidence that the Pharisees were formed into a brotherhood, but this was never as strict as that of the Essenes. In one of his earlier works (*Quod Omnis Probus Liber*), Philo of Alexandria has a great deal to tell us about

them. Our information is supplemented by numerous
references in the writings of Josephus. They shared with
the Pharisees a horror of giving allegiance to any king
except God Himself, and *c.* 21 B.C. Herod the Great excused
both them and the Pharisees from making to him any
formal oath of allegiance. They took vows of celibacy,
but adopted other people's children and brought them up
in their beliefs. One sect, however, followed a custom of
trial marriages, the period lasting for three years. If in
this interval a child was born, then the marriage was
formally ratified. It is probable that this kind of thing
was not usual amongst them, but was customary in some
decadent group, for their general attitude was one of
extreme asceticism. They lived in brotherhoods and had
all things in common. They had no buying or selling
amongst themselves, but had a common fund administered
by elected stewards. They had hostels in various cities,
where there lived one of their members whose duty it was
to make provision for Essene travellers. They pitied all
men, and fed the needy.

The Essenes attached great importance to ceremonial
purity. They bathed before each meal, and wore linen
garments which were of necessity of vegetable products
and so could not be 'unclean' because of any association
with dead animals. They elected a 'priest' who should
cook their meals. Ordinary cleansing customs were not
clean enough for the Essenes, so that they offered their own
sacrifices instead of joining in the sacrifices at the Temple.
It is said that they sent gifts, though not blood-gifts, but
did not appear themselves. They were most strict in
receiving members into their Order, and would-be initiates
had to spend four years on probation of one type and
another. Then, before touching the common food, they
swore oaths to reverence God, to observe justice to all
men, to hate the wicked and to help the just. They swore
to be loyal to authority and never themselves to abuse their

power, to love truth and to abhor falsehood, to keep body and soul clean and pure in every way, and to reveal no secrets of their brotherhood to the uninitiated. They are said in the main to have confined their work to husbandry, though Josephus says that after they had prayed to the sun (a strange custom peculiar to them), each man was sent away by his superior to exercise such craft as he was skilled to perform. Their home was beyond Jordan in the desert country, and altogether it is very easy to draw parallels between this strict ascetic order, with its ideas of brotherhood and monasticism, and various Christian communal experiments of these and other days.

We are here in the midst of the times of the Gospel, and in these various groups and sects we find traces of all those elements which we have discussed. We still have the clash between Separatism and Universalism, between the Hebrew and the Greek way of life. We have those whose worldly wisdom led them wholly away from thoughts of the Kingdom of God, and those whose zeal for the Kingdom led them into every kind of peril and persecution. For some of them the Law was still a schoolmaster to lead them to God, whilst for others it had crystallised into a hard legalism which became an end in itself. The Jew still to-day, as in the time of Jesus, and since the time of his Persian overlords, has to fight against alien influences if he would hold his own; and it still seems to be true now, as always, that his separate identity depends upon his insistence on those things which belong peculiarly to Jewry.

LIST OF KINGS

PTOLEMAID EMPIRE (EGYPT)

	B.C.
Ptolemy I (Soter I)	311–283/2
Ptolemy II (Philadelphos) . . .	285–246
Ptolemy III (Euergetes I) . . .	246–221
Ptolemy IV (Philopator) . . .	221–203
Ptolemy V (Epiphanes) . . .	203–181/0
Ptolemy VI (Philometor) . . .	181/0–145
Ptolemy (VII) Euergetes II, Physcon) .	145–116
Ptolemy VIII (Soter II, Lathyros) .	116–108/7 and 88–80
Ptolemy IX (Alexander I) . . .	108/7–88
Ptolemy X (Alexander II) . . .	80
Ptolemy XI (Auletes)	80–51
Ptolemy XII and Cleopatra VII . .	51–48
Ptolemy XIII and Cleopatra VII	47–44
Ptolemy XIV (Caesar) and Cleopatra VII	44–30

THE HASMONAEANS

	B.C.
Judas Maccabaeus	166/5–160
Jonathan (High Priest) . . .	160/59–142/1
Simon (High Priest)	142/1–135/4
John Hyrcanus I (High Priest, King) .	134/3–104/3
Aristobulus I (High Priest, King) . .	103/2
Alexander Jannaeus (High Priest, King) .	102/1–76/5
Alexandra Salome	75/4–67/6
Hyrcanus II (High Priest) . . .	75/4–66/5 and 63–40
Aristobulus II (High Priest, King) . .	66/5–63
Antigonus (High Priest, King) . .	40–37
Herod the Great	37–4

PERSIAN EMPIRE

	B.C.
Cyrus	538–529
Cambyses	529–522
Darius I (Hystaspis)	522–486
Xerxes I	485–465
Artaxerxes I (Longimanus) . . .	464–424
Xerxes II (few months only) . .	424–423
Darius II (Nothus)	423–404
Artaxerxes II (Mnemon) . . .	404–359
Artaxerxes III (Ochus) . . .	359–338
Darius III (Codomannus) . . .	338–331

SELEUCID EMPIRE

	B.C.
Seleucus I (Nicator)	311–281/0
Antiochus I (Soter)	280–262/1
Antiochus II (Theos)	261/0–247/6
Seleucus II (Kallinikos) . . .	246/5–226/5
Seleucus III (Keraunos) . . .	225/4–223
Antiochus III (The Great) . . .	223–187
Seleucus IV (Philopator) . . .	187–175
Antiochus IV (Epiphanes) . . .	175–163
Antiochus V (Eupator) . . .	163–162
Demetrius I (Soter)	162–150
Alexander Balas	150–145
Demetrius II (Nicator) . . .	145–139/8
Antiochus VI (Epiphanes) . . .	145–142/1
Tryphon 142/1–138	
Antiochus VII (Euergetes, Sidetes) .	139/8–129
Demetrius II (Nicator) . . .	129–126/5
Antiochus VIII (Grypos) . . .	125–96
Antiochus IX (Kyzikenos) . . .	115–95

(Confusion with rival claimants for the next 30 years).

RULERS OF JUDÆA FROM B.C. 4 TO FALL OF JERUSALEM A.D. 70

Archelaus	B.C. 4–A.D.6.

(Procurators)	A.D.
Coponius	6–9
Marcus Ambibulus . . c.	9–12
Annus Rufus . . . c.	12–15
Valerius Gratus . . .	15–26
Pontius Pilate . . .	26–36
Marcellus . . .	36
Marullus . . .	37
Merennius Capito . .	?–41
Herod Agrippa I . .	41–44
Cuspius Fadus . . .	44–?
Tiberius Alexander . .	?
Cumanus . . .	?48–52
Felix	52–? 60
Porcius Festus . . .	?60–62
Albinus . . .	63–64
Gessius Florus . . .	64–

INDEX

BC
AD

100

100

200

198

168
167 Maccabaean revolt
166

Ptolemies (Egypt) control Palestine

Seleucids (Syria) begin control Palestine

Antiochus IV (175-163) issues his edict

100

200